C'MERE AND I
TELL YA . . .

The 2 Johnnies are the hugely popular comedians Johnny B (O'Brien) and Johnny Smacks (McMahon). From Tipperary, they were brought together by a love of music, comedy and GAA. They are the hosts of the phenomenally popular *2 Johnnies Podcast*. Together they have had nine number-one singles, as well as a sold-out live tour.

C'MERE AND I TELL YA . . .

THE 2 JOHNNIES' GUIDE TO IRISH LIFE

Johnny B and Johnny Smacks

SANDYCOVE

an imprint of

PENGUIN BOOKS

SANDYCOVE
UK | USA | Canada | Ireland | Australia
India | New Zealand | South Africa

Sandycove is part of the Penguin Random House group of companies
whose addresses can be found at global.penguinrandomhouse.com.

First published 2020
001

Copyright © Johnny O'Brien and Johnny McMahon, 2020

The moral right of the authors has been asserted

Typeset by Kazoo Independent Publishing Services Ltd.
Printed and bound in Great Britain by Clays Ltd, Elcograf S.p.A.

A CIP catalogue record for this book is available from the British Library

ISBN: 978-1-844-88508-4

www.greenpenguin.co.uk

CONTENTS

INTRODUCTION

Compton, South LA. The sun is splitting the concrete. It must be a million degrees – we can't understand the American thermometer on our rental car. We've been pumping tunes on the drive over: Dr Dre, Snoop Dogg and, of course, 'Straight Outta Compton'. But we turn down the music once we get there. The longer we go unnoticed the better. One of the most famous cities in the world, Compton has a population of just 97,000 people – more than 25,000 fewer than Cork – but everyone's heard of it, and not necessarily for good reasons.

Our new friend is taking us to his neighbourhood, where they're having a barbecue. As we walk with him, there are two particularly angry dogs trying to eat us through a fence, music is drifting from the apartment building across the street, and there are people everywhere. Someone shouts, 'Who called the police?' (We're the only two white guys on the street.) They all laugh. The guy relaxes when he sees we're with a local, but he clarifies, 'I ain't saying you look like po-lice, but you is what po-lice look like.' He greets our friend with one of those handshakes only Americans can pull off.

Our camera crew for the TV show we are filming arrives and is treated to some very tasty pork ribs, cooked on a barbecue made from the bonnet of an old pick-up truck. It's like the set of that movie *Boys in the Hood*. We chat with our host about the reputation Compton and Watts have. It can't be that bad here, really, can it? He politely but strongly advises that we don't come back at night. It was like the place had vampires.

'What happens at night?' we ask.

'I don't even wanna say.'

We drive to where Dr Dre went to school. Our director suggests we pull up and get some footage there, but our guide says, 'Ahmm, actually, maybe don't stop. Just shoot out the window.'

'There'll be no shooting out the window here,' we say.

He can take a joke. He takes us to the train station, where there's a big cool sign that says COMPTON. A fight breaks out and we tip on to the next spot, a drive-thru funeral home. They tell us it reduces the chances of gang attacks.

JB: *I don't know if you still shake hands there or beep the horn or what. I want a chicken roll, so we stop at some giant supermarket, where I buy a roll and some cooked chicken. There's an awful queue for the checkout. Americans love queuing. The fella before me puts 8 gallons of cranberry juice on the conveyor belt. 'Jaysus, lad, have you a kidney infection?' I joke, but he doesn't understand me. I'd say I'm as well off – he's too busy loading up his trolley with whiskey. It must be an LA thing; I've never seen anyone mix Jameson and cranberry juice at home. His load includes more liquor than one person is allowed to buy, and the cashier has* *to call the manager. Your man with the kidney infection freaks out. Christ, all I wanted was a chicken roll. There'll be murder here. The manager takes the whiskey man to another till, and I'm out the gap. The whole film crew are parked outside waiting for me. I thought I'd only be two minutes, like in Spar at home. I apologize to our cameraman. He's from New York and they all seem pretty into sandwiches up there, so he's bemused by my breaded chicken, block of butter and foot-long roll.*

It's our first time making a TV show. We don't know what the craic is with stopping for tea and goujons. There's a lot we don't know the craic with, to be honest. Travelling with us are two producers, an assistant producer, cameramen, a sound man, a director and our Compton tour guide, and then there are the two of us, the 'stars' of the show. Four years ago we started making sketches on our phones and now here we are, filming in the city of Compton, County LA. We're not saying that to make it sound like County LA should be in the All-Ireland. It's actually a county, and it's the setting for the first episode of our first ever TV show. We pull up at the Compton courthouse and ask our guide if he's been called up here before.

He says, 'Oh yeah.'

'For what?' we inquire.

'Ahmm . . . parking tickets.'

It's a long way to Tipperary, but it's an even longer way to Compton.

2020 has been a crazy year for everyone, including us. If you've just picked up this book in your local bookshop and are wondering if you should buy this work of art or not, we insist you do! It's been a tough year and you deserve it, and so do we. And it's a class book if we may say so ourselves.

We started 2020 with our world tour, which kicked off in Australia. G'day, mate! On the way home from Oz, there was a quick stopover in Austria for the Today FM ski trip – pure mayhem. Then we packed our bags and headed for the home of the free, land of the brave. No, not Carlow, the USA! We were going to spend a month in the States making a TV show as well as performing live across the country as part of our world tour. Now, I know what you're thinking: how did two lads from Tipp manage to fool everyone into this and make a decent career for themselves? Well, you're about to find out. We hope this book will give you a glimpse into the craziness that goes on in our minds and into how we got to be the men we are today. So if you want to hear about trying to get the shift at a teenage disco, or how not to be a disastrous debs date, or the inside scoop on pulling off a local fundraiser, then this is the book for you. Pull up a stool, pour yourself a cold one. C'mere and I tell ya!

P.S. this is a disclaimer, kind of like at the start of *Law and Order* or *Judge Judy*: The names and places in some of the stories you're about to read have been changed to protect the people involved. Basically they're our friends and we don't want to ruin them.

If that doesn't make ya want to read this book, then we don't know what will. Enjoy!

Big love,
The 2 Johnnies.

TEENAGE DISCOS

Ah, teenage discos, ya have to love them. Strangely enough, we must be the only people in Ireland who've attended teenage discos as adults (not in a weird, creepy way, stick with us, all will be explained). When we first started The 2 Johnnies, we got an email asking us to come to a teenage disco to make a personal appearance. Personal appearances were a big deal at the time, made famous by glamour model Jordan and the cast of *Jersey Shore*. Even the cast of *Tallafornia* were paid to show up to places (*Tallafornia* was Ireland's answer to *Jersey Shore*, but it was set in Tallaght. If you haven't seen it, just google it. You can thank us later. It's hilarious, although it's not meant to be a comedy). All these so-called celebrities were getting in on the act and making a fortune. We thought we were on the pig's back, that we'd hit the big time. Did this mean we were celebrities now? We'd seen clips of these appearances online and they looked like paradise. There was champagne flowing, palm trees, cordoned-off VIP areas and big, burly bouncers who looked like they'd take the head off ya. We were buzzing, thinking our personal appearance would be like this. It wasn't.

Those clips we'd seen online were of celebrities

dancing to Calvin Harris in a flashy Ibiza nightclub; we were heading to the bright lights and tropical surroundings of our local nightclub in Cahir, County Tipperary. There was certainly no champagne or palm trees around, and the bouncers were more interested in who was going to win the 7.45 horse race at Kempton than they were in us. They did have a VIP area – well, sort of. It consisted of three high-visibility railings set up around us, which, may we add, we had to carry into the venue ourselves under the watchful eye of the event organizer, who, to be honest, looked like a villain out of *Love/Hate*. If he left us short a few quid at the end of the night we weren't going to be arguing with him. I bet the cast of *Love Island* don't have to put up with this. Also, the high-vis railings looked awfully familiar. If we were to hazard a guess, we'd say they were stolen from the council, which was carrying out roadworks in the locality that week. If we had two shovels in our hands, we'd have been mistaken for maintenance men.

We arrived in before there were any teenagers inside, and we couldn't help but throw out a few dance moves like we were fifteen again. We couldn't believe how small the kids were when they started milling in. When we were fifteen, lads had moustaches. Then the room was full as a biscuit tin, and the smoke machine was turned up to full blast. When the music started, it was mayhem. Eventually after an hour of awkwardly posing for photos and being heckled by schoolkids, we got out of Dodge. On our way out, we passed a young lad heading into the disco, casually supping from a can of Dutch Gold. We looked at each other and thought, *Surely teenage discos weren't like this in our day, or were they . . . ?*

Teenage discos are a magical time in a teenager's life. You usually go to your first disco aged twelve and enjoy them right through till you're around sixteen, although it's hard to make up your mind about what age you need to stop going. It's like an unwritten rule: you don't go to teenage discos after your sixteenth birthday. But a friend of ours really took the piss with this rule. Let's call him Shane, because that's his actual name. We don't care; we will name and shame. He deserves it. Shane had his mind made up for him by our local bouncer, who had copped on to Shane's unusual habit of rocking up to the teenage disco on a Friday night and the local nightclub on the Saturday. He was the only fella who was asked for ID going to a teenage disco. The bouncer said, 'Hey, kid, it's time to shit or get off the pot. It's one or the other. Make your mind up.' The same bouncer worked at both places so the jig was up for Shane and he managed to get barred from both places. Not his finest moment.

JS: The excitement and hype surrounding the disco always started at the beginning of the week, when the inevitable question was: 'Are you going to Meka?' Meka was the local disco in Nenagh I frequented as a teenager, where I had many unsuccessful liaisons with the opposite sex. So when the follow-up question – 'Who are you gonna shift at the disco?' – was asked,

I normally played my cards close to my chest, because I was shite with women.

The first disco I ever went to was a foam party. Sounds glamorous. It's not. The foam is made from Windolene, which left the floor of the nightclub squeaky clean but burnt the eyes out of everyone's head. It also ruined my suede shoes. Yes, that's right, I wore suede shoes to a teenage disco. Fashion was important at these events, so I had to seek advice from someone whose opinion I valued. Donatella Versace? Brendan Courtney? Dennis who works in the local menswear shop in Roscrea? Nope, I took advice from the one person I could trust – none other than . . . my mother. In hindsight, not my best idea. My brown suede shoes were paired with brown cords and a cream shirt. In my head I looked like Enrique Iglesias but in reality I looked like an OAP looking forward to some social dancing at a Jimmy Buckley concert. If you think I was bad, my friend Joe liked my look so much he bought the exact same outfit but in black. To this day he's still called the Priest.

It was always left to me to provide the lifts to and from the disco, as my mother was deemed the coolest parent. We would beg her to drop us a half-mile down to road to avoid everyone seeing four of us climb out of her Fiat Cinquecento, which was like a clown car it was so small. Even as teenagers we almost had to fold ourselves in half to get into it. Of course she always insisted on driving us right to the door. Safety first. This wasn't the most embarrassing thing she put me through at a disco, though. The worst was when she gatecrashed the disco. My ma worked in the shop in our local school, so she knew everybody who went to the disco and was always curious about what we got up to at them. One night curiosity got the better of her and she decided to take a look for herself. As Fatman Scoop pumped over the speakers, I was doing what every fourteen-year-old lad does – trying to get the shift. I was chatting to a girl in my year and was about to seal the deal when she uttered the following words to me: 'Is that your mother over there?' I looked across the dance floor and was shocked to see my mother boogying away with my friends, who all thought this was hilarious. I legged it over and frog-marched her out the door. Any hope of getting the shift was out the window thanks to word spreading like wildfire that 'Johnny McMahon brought his mother to the disco.' Ah, the embarrassment! I'm going bright red even writing this.

Like it or not, what seems to go hand in hand with teenage discos is underage drinking. Like tea in a mug.

Disclaimer: **If you're reading this book and you're under eighteen, underage drinking is bad. On the other hand, if you're over eighteen, then you've definitely watered down your parents' vodka at one stage or another, or shared a can of cider with your mate in a bush somewhere. We know we have.**

We don't condone underage drinking, so here are some tips for the parents:

- **If your kids arrive home from a disco and declare their undying love for you while dancing around the kitchen with the dog – they're pissed.**

- If they go through a full packet of Airwaves chewing gum, they do not have congestion problems – they're pissed.

- If they have lost their keys, phone, wallet and one of their shoes, they were not mugged – they're pissed.

- If you find them sleeping in the porch, they didn't 'think it would be comfortable' – they're pissed.

- If they come home with a random sheep they've adopted as the new family pet, they have not decided they want to be a farmer – they're pissed.

- If their friend calls you to say your child is staying with them for the night, they're not getting an early start on a school project the next day – they're pissed (but they have good mates).

JS: When I first started going to discos in Club Meka, they had a strict no-drinking policy. How did they enforce that, I hear you ask? Well, the bouncers had a trick up their sleeve. The breath test. Before you were allowed in, you had to give the bouncer a breath sample by blowing in his face. Obviously breathalysers must not have been invented by the early noughties, but these bouncers didn't need them anyway; they had snouts on them like airport sniffer dogs and no one messed with them. I genuinely felt sorry for them one night when I gave them a breath sample after having a feed of garlic mushrooms ten minutes beforehand. I'd say they nearly got sick. The joke was on me in the end – no one gets a shift with garlic breath.

But not to be deterred by the bouncers' ability to spot who had been drinking, at age fifteen myself and my friend Robert experimented with a naggin of vodka. I talked Robert into trying it first. He took the biggest gulp I'd ever seen. Phil Mitchell in *EastEnders* would have been proud of him. No sooner had poor Robert swallowed this liquid poison than it re-emerged from his nose, followed by projectile vomit (thankfully none of it got on my suede shoes). We both agreed that vodka wasn't for us. So instead we shared a bottle of Bacardi Breezer between us. Pure rock stars. When we arrived at the disco, the bouncers smelled the vodka from a mile off and turned us away. The vomit wouldn't have helped things either.

JB: *If you're hard enough or live in a town that's loose enough, you'll be drinking at fourteen. In our town there was a publican who had kind of given up, stopped showering and listened to a lot of Lynyrd Skynyrd. He didn't seem to care that his pub was a bit rundown and had started to smell like a fiddler's armpit. He was busy keeping his eyelids open and the rats away. He'd a head on him like a pumpkin carved for Halloween that you'd left out in the sun, and checking for ID was way down his list of priorities.*

We went in one day for a game of pool. We tried to chat to him but he was busy staring at a fly on the counter. We played away.

'Can you turn on the jukebox, Pat?' I asked.

'I suppose,' he grunted.

When he got up off the stool, I'd swear I saw sand fall from his shoulders. 'Twas like watching a mummy come alive in the movies. God knows how long he'd been sitting there.

'A pint while you're up, Pat?' chanced my friend.

The pint arrived and Pat accepted the fiver, returning the change without eye contact. Good thing too, as we were in our school uniforms! We zipped up our jackets and started talking about what a hard day it had been at the office and about how that boss of ours was some prick. Sure, you'd need a pint after a day like that. I don't know whether Pat heard our performance or if he cared, but we had a pub that would serve us and that was gold.

On the night of the next teenage disco, we put on our shirts and headed in the back door of Pat's. 'Twas like being in an undercover spy movie, trying to stay cool. We got served two pints each and headed down to the disco. You can't imagine how hard we felt, three of us walking down the hill like the feckin' Bee Gees. A few girls from our school had heard we were getting served (we told them) and they asked if we could get them drink.

'Ya of course, no problem, girl. What do ye want?'

When they said, 'Two West Coast Coolers between the four of us,' we nearly fell down laughing, thinking we were like Shane MacGowan at this stage. My oldest-looking mate got them the bottles and we were surely in pole position for the shift once we all went inside.

Up to the door, ladies first.

When we got to the door, the bouncer took one look at us and said, 'Ye've been drinking! Out!'

The girls laughed back at us as they strutted inside. I heard the girl my older mate was after shifted a lad from Ardfinnan in the disco. My mate head-butted him after, but that's a different story. The moral of the story is *underage drinking is not cool and won't get you the shift.*

We went back to Pat's the following Saturday, bringing a new friend. New guy wasn't able to hold his drink and after one pint he spotted the dartboard, picked up the darts and fired his first throw into the air vent in the ceiling. Without looking up from his paper, Pat said, 'Ye can head away now, lads.'

When you've finally navigated the bouncers and entered the disco, that's when the fun really starts. There's normally one thing on all hormone-addled teenagers' minds, and we were no different. That one thing is 'the shift'. In Tipperary we always called it 'shifting', although seemingly nowadays the cool kids are calling it 'meeting', which for us just doesn't have the same panache. While doing our research on this (ya, we know what you're thinking – there's no way ye two do research. Well, wash your mouth out. We're professionals . . . sometimes) it came to light that in Cork people would say, 'Will you go with my friend?' Trust the People's Republic of Cork to do it differently. God knows what they say in Carlow. Anyway, the dictionary according to The 2 Johnnies would define the shift as follows:

THE SHIFT: a word that is used to describe a French kiss in Ireland. Basically it's where two people wear the face off each other until one person gets lockjaw or the spit puddle becomes too much for the parties involved.

Examples: 'Ah, lads, he got the shift last night', 'Will you shift my friend?'

SYNONYMS: meet, go with, kiss, neck on, score (mainly used by posh Dublin people), tonguing, snogging, tonsil hockey, canoodling, making out.

JB: *The first teenage disco I went to, I found it fairly daunting. There were lads there that I didn't know from school. They were from The Other Village, like the dark place in* The Lion King *where you must never go. I saw a lad from our school in deep shift mode, sucking the face off some girl, his two hands absolutely welded to her arse. Because he was cool out, he was wearing baggy tracksuit pants. Another fella walked up and pulled the lad's tracksuit pants down to his ankles, and God love him, wasn't he on his first boner. The girl he was shifting was mortified, and then as he bent down to pull his pants back up, he nearly head-butted her. I lived in fear when I left the house without a belt for years after this. Scarred for life.*

But the most intimidating thing of all was women. Well, girls. I'd gone to an all-boys primary school and my interactions with females my own age were limited to the rare occasion we'd kick a ball into their school and have to retrieve it like navy seals. That and when my cousins came to visit, but we're not that kind of family. Walking up to an unfamiliar girl and talking to her was impossible. I'd have a better chance of winning the World Cup – Shane Long doing the running and me there for the tap in. Nice one. The way to do it was you'd get your friend to ask her, 'Will you shift my friend?' She'd have to decide in that split second as she tried to judge if you were a lunatic or not, at the same time trying to get a glimpse of you over your mate's shoulder.

If you made eye contact, you'd both burst into flames. At my first disco, I asked my mate Slick if he'd ask that nice-looking wan if she'd shift me. I couldn't bear the tension; 'twas like waiting for the X Factor results. I went to the jacks (I didn't really need to go), and when I came back, Slick would have an answer.

'Give it to me straight, lad.'

'She said no.'

'Grand,' says I. 'Didn't like her anyway. The boys said she smells of bleach.'

We repeated the routine. I headed into the jacks again.

Slick had more bad news.

'Grand,' says I. 'Didn't like her either. Heard she has webbed feet.'

He nodded in agreement. It did seem like a strange coincidence when Slick ended up dating both of those girls afterwards. They don't call him Slick for not'n. I went home shiftless and he's married to one of them now. I should never have gone to the jacks.

Arriving at the disco can be quite daunting. There are so many different types of people you'll encounter there. We've all met them, but which one were you?

WHITE-TRACKSUIT MAN: This guy was to be avoided at all costs. He was normally found doing a weird dance with his hands behind his back. Think *Young Offenders*. He always wore white socks and tucked his tracksuit bottoms into them. He was to be approached with caution as he had the capacity to dish out black eyes at a second's notice. Odds are he's in jail now.

MR BREAKDANCER: There was always one big shot

who reckoned he could breakdance. He'd watched too many Take That videos as a child and practised dance moves in his room at home. Now he's most likely in a comedy duo who are also podcasters and have a TV show. Probably called something stupid like The 2 Johnn . . . wait . . . shit, that was me. You can decide which of us was Mr Breakdancer. Answers on a postcard.

THE MEAN GIRLS: These cool chicks were normally found wearing ra-ra skirts and snow boots. They were the type who peaked in secondary school, the cool kids who everyone was afraid to talk to or stand up to. Most likely working in your local deli now.

THE SNACK MAN: We all had that one friend who only went to the disco to visit the tuck shop. They were completely oblivious to anything that was happening at the disco. They never danced and sat happily in the corner, munching on Rancheros and Picnic bars, washing it all down with a bottle of Score. Probably works in computers nowadays.

THE SMOKERS: These people paid the admission price yet never set foot on the dance floor. They spent all their time outside in the smoking area sponging cigarettes from everyone. When it was time to head home they'd douse themselves in perfume or Lynx to mask the smell from Mammy and Daddy. Could be dead by now or they're that person at work who has to have a smoke break every twenty minutes.

THE ACCOMPLICE: Also known as the wingman/ woman. Their main duties included asking random people 'Will you shift my friend?' as is tradition at teenage discos. Normally a very unselfish person. Probably working in sales now due to their persuasiveness and ability to get the job done.

THE SERIAL SHIFTERS: They had an amazing ability to always get the shift. They were very rarely seen at the disco, as they spent most of the time on the shifting couches, normally located upstairs, where you don't want to ever find your sons or daughters. The serial shifters are possibly porn stars by now, or at least operating their own Only Fans account.

Here's how our escapades at the disco usually went:

Johnny Smacks' Diary
of a Disco Kid

5.00 p.m. Begin preparation

As Roy Keane once said, 'Fail to prepare, prepare to fail.' He was probably talking about the World Cup, but the same applies to a teenage disco. The preparation mostly revolves around getting a shift. The approach we took was to text every girl in our phonebook that we knew was heading to the disco and put in the groundwork. 'Well, what u up 2?' was the standard message. It never worked but we wouldn't let that knock us off our stride.

5.30 p.m. Fuel the body

It's important to build up your energy levels before the main event. The key thing to remember is not to eat anything that will give you bad breath. Obviously avoid garlic and Taytos. They're a disaster, altogether. No amount of chewing gum will mask the smell of them. Also, getting a bit of food in is handy when you're having a sneaky can of cider between six of you. Ya gotta line the stomach.

6.00 p.m. Get fresh

Break out the Lynx Africa or rob your father's Old Spice, because it's time to get beautified. Our beauty regime when heading to a disco was simple. For starters, we liked to cover our bodies head to toe in Lynx, until it was almost difficult to breathe. Then came a hefty dollop of Brylcreem, and by hefty we mean half a tub. The hair wasn't complete until your fringe was spiked so high you could almost receive signal from RTÉ. The hair also had to be rock-hard to the touch, so that it took an hour to wash out. For extra va-va-voom, you'd top it off with a spray of Old Spice, so you too smelled like a middle-aged farmer from Navan. Finally, at least ten minutes were spent gargling mouthwash, while giving yourself a last-minute pep talk in the mirror. You've got this!

7.00 p.m. Join the queue

Why were queues for discos so long? It wasn't as if the local gangster who was organizing it wasn't going to take the €12 from you. The queue is the perfect opportunity to get chatting to the opposite sex. We didn't, though, because our mams would make us stay in the car until the queue had died down. Thanks for that, Mammies.

8.30 p.m. Enter the disco

It's time to peacock. It's essential that you look as cool as possible on your walk in. We used to go for the American gangster-rap walk, which involved a slight hobble and swaying arms. We thought we looked cool like Snoop Dogg. In reality we looked like a group of lads who miraculously all managed to sprain their ankles at the same time. For women it was a chance to strut their stuff. We've seen less-sassy struts on Milan catwalks than we have on the dance floors of Tipperary. You go, girl!

9.05 p.m. Find where your crew stand

Boys on one side and girls on the other was the way it was in our parents' time, but when we were going to teenage discos, it was about each town/village having their own spot in the venue.

JS: All the tough lads from Nenagh occupied the back wall. It was their home turf. We stood under the stairs – nice quiet lads, not wanting to get involved in any trouble; just happy to be there and soak up the atmosphere.

9.15 p.m. Offload your jacket

Did your parents always make you wear a jacket to the disco even though it was a wall-to-wall sweatbox? Yep, us too. Here's a tip: make friends with the DJ. If he likes you, it's likely he'll let you leave your jacket in the DJ box. This is handy for three reasons:

1. It saves you having to pay €2 for the cloakroom.

2. You avoid all the queues for said cloakroom at the end of the disco.

3. Most importantly, you look cool as fuck if people think you're friends with the DJ, cos he's the coolest person at the disco.

9.35 p.m. Go for a lap

'Going for a lap' is a term used nationwide by disco-goers young and old. It basically means you walk around the disco with your group of friends to survey the goings-on, trying to work out who's single and who's not. It's like an animal stalking its prey, but while animals are on the hunt for the next meal, we were on the hunt for the next shift.

10.30 p.m. Go for a lap again

You didn't have any luck the first time, so it's time for round 2.

11.00 p.m. Go for one last lap

Yep, you guessed it, time for round 3.

11.30 p.m. Disco ends

There's only one way to end the night and that's with one last song. Beyoncé? Akon? Cotton Eye Joe? Nope. You link arms with the nearest person to you and, hands on hearts, the whole dancefloor stands to attention as 'Amhrán na bhFiann', our national anthem, belts out over the speakers. Only in Ireland.

11.45 p.m. Refuel again

Some top athletes refuel with a protein shake, but that will not suffice after dancing to Scooter for almost three hours. You need to replenish the body, and nothing does that better than a feed from Supermac's. That was where the unofficial after-party for all teenage discos was held. Come to think of it, we've seen more shifting in Supermac's than we have in nightclubs. There's no better way to top off the night than a taco chip. Other takeaways are available; we just really love taco chips.

12.00 a.m. Interrogation time

For me, once we got into the car, it was time to mentally prepare for a barrage of questions from my mother. I swear she should have been a detective. We'd start off with some general small talk, but within minutes she'd manage to get us all tied up in our lies. She's Roscrea's answer to Jessica Fletcher.

Looking back on it all, we remember turning sixteen and being heartbroken that for us the teenage disco experience was over and it was time to face the big bad world. As adults we dipped our toe back into the scene, but we knew it wasn't for us. Following on from our disastrous outing in Cahir, we got offered another PA at a disco. This time it was in the Las Vegas of north Tipperary – Nenagh.

JS: It was like coming full circle for me. It's quite romantic in a way that I started my teenage disco years there and that's where they would come to an end.

Foolishly we didn't learn our lesson from the last

PA and agreed to do another one. This time we were assured that the bouncers would actually give a shite about our safety and that of the disco-goers, but there were still no palm trees or champagne. In fairness, though, this one was better organized. The teens queued two by two for photos with us like we were nineties popstars. We were thinking this is all too good to be true. And it was.

The last two young lads approached us for a photo, and one of them said, 'Hey, Johnny B, do you know my mother? Her name is P—'

'Ah yeah, I know her,' Johnny B replied awkwardly.

'She said you're always texting her.'

'Ah ya, just about *work* is all.' Johnny B was sweating at this stage.

'That's not what she said,' said the young lad, and he took a selfie.

We're getting too old for this shit, we thought.

And with that, we collected our few bob and headed straight for the nearest pub, licking our wounds after being roasted by a thirteen-year-old kid. As we sat perched on the high stools in the Kenyon bar, we vowed to one another that that was it for us and teenage discos.

SCHOOL

JS: People used to tell me your school days are the best days of your life, but I didn't believe them until I started getting quotes for car insurance. Looking back, in school all I had to worry about was putting copious amounts of Brylcreem in my hair and making sure I had €3.50 for a chicken roll at lunch.

Surviving my first day of secondary school was definitely the most daunting thing I've ever done in my life, though. There was some amount of shoe-staring going on. I was too nervous to lift my head and make eye contact with anyone. Almost as if by keeping my head down I'd become invisible and no one would bother me. I'd come from a country school and didn't know many people in my year. Now we were in with the big bad townies. Even though I lived in town, I didn't class myself as a townie. They were hardy boys and I was a teddy bear. In an attempt to ease the first-day nerves and general anxiety in the room, the principal said, 'Ye're gonna be here for the next five to six years, so get on with it.'

I was thinking, *Fuck, this is like San Quentin Prison.*

He didn't instil much confidence in me that I'd last the first day, never mind six years.

On my first day I brought all my books, every one of them. It turned out all we needed was a notepad. I was carrying more than a soldier in Afghanistan. If anyone had pushed me, I'd have toppled over. I was bent over from carrying the bag. There were no classes that day, just people telling us how miserable the next few years were going to be.

I had my tie real tight, like I was going to a wedding. The mother had done it up and insisted it was to be tight. I could barely swallow. The older lads in the corridors didn't approve of my look and were shouting, 'Ah, sham boys, look at the innocent boy with the tie on!'

I remember my first lunch break. I was so scared. The bell rang for break, and then in a split second it was every man for himself. It was like the bull run in Pamplona; there were bodies everywhere, bags flying, anything to aid you in the quest to get to the top of the queue at the canteen. I've seen people getting broke up over a place in that queue. If you stood still, the career guidance teacher would stand on top of you. Even the teachers took no prisoners.

Some boys used to treat this lunchtime rush as a sport. They'd watch people rushing along the corridor and fire schoolbags at their legs. It was like a slide tackle from Roy Keane. Lads would be getting wiped out by a 25 kg school bag. 'Ah sham, look at the innocent boy falling over his legs.' At Halloween it'd be worse. They'd throw Black Cats at you. What kind of lunatics were they, throwing bangers around school?

Along with the lunatics, there were lots of other types in school, and you were put into a group whether you liked it or not. Were you a jock, Johnny?

JB: *A jock? This isn't* American Pie.

JS: In our school we had:

- The Korn Dudes, who were into heavy metal and always seemed angry at the world as they trudged around school in their black hoodies, writing band names on the cubicle doors of the gents' toilets.

- The Hardy Bucks, who loved to smoke on school grounds and shout 'Sketch!' when a teacher was coming. They usually weren't big on sport and rarely took part in PE. These were the people who ended up in huge fights after school that were the talk of the school for weeks. Also, they were probably out drinking most weekends.

- The Fridgets. If you weren't shifting loads and acting up (basically, if you were nice), you could be labelled frigid. School is harsh.

- The Hunz were a group of girls I found quite scary. They were fond of the odd cigarette in the jacks at breaktime and thought applying four layers of foundation was a good look. It wasn't.

JB: *My school was quite similar to yours, although it was less* American Pie. *It wasn't quite* Sing Street *or* The Breakfast Club *either, if we're making a habit of comparing our schools to film titles. It was a big mixed vocational school at the foot of the Galtee Mountains, formed when the Christian Brothers, the convent and the local tech all came together as one school – a recipe for disaster and mayhem. Our school had students from all the neighbouring parishes. Less than ten miles from* *our school was a large fee-paying school, the type of school where the students spoke eloquently and actually pronounced their th's. Ours was a lot rougher around the edges. We could barely manage conversational English, never mind worry about elocution. Red sauce was the speciality in our canteen. The whiteboard that displayed the menu said SAUSAGE ROLL, but if you ate one, you'd still be tasting the ketchup at Mass on Sunday.*

By the time my mate Gonzo and I were in sixth year, we were the only two lads left bringing in our own lunch. For some reason lots of first and second years did it, but after that people thought they were too cool for the lunch box. We didn't, plus we just loved sandwiches – ham every day of the week for the two of us. (Gonzo brought tuna once but instantly regretted it – pure stink.) During our summer holidays, we worked on building sites and always brought sandwiches, so we thought nothing of it. Some cool kid slagged Gonzo about the lunch box one day and he got a box in the jaw for his trouble. We were bringing lunch boxes back into fashion.

Gangs of lads used to spend their lunch in the toilets. As an adult I've got to know the man who looks after the school and he's sound, but he has a lot to answer for, because when I was in school there was a fair bang of meat factory boning hall off those jacks. And fellas would spend their only free time there, standing around, talking rubbish in a constant smell of urine. How does it make sense?

'Hey, I need to have a chat with you.'

'Ya no bother. Let's stand beside a load of random lads pissing and see how we get on.'

Fellas are animals.

The real crayon-eaters would roll up a ball of toilet paper, wet it in the sink (or sometimes the toilet) and throw the soaked ball up so it stuck to the ceiling. The jacks ceiling looked like the surface of the moon. A few hardy glue-sniffers would kick in the cubicle doors while lads were on the job. One monster even pulled a sink off the wall. I think he joined the army after. God help whoever invades Ireland if they meet him.

JS: I went to a mixed vocational school, so we had the girls to worry about too. It's no surprise that I had my first taste of love there. Teenage love: you think it's going to last forever until you're in your bedroom listening to 'Lonely' by Akon. No one forgets their first love. Mine was a girl in my class. I must have been in second year at the time, and for the whole day I used to just stare at her. Then she'd look back and I'd look away. It was butterflies, I guess, although it meant I never learned a thing in double history. Whenever I looked at her, I heard Westlife playing in my head. I never had a notion what our homework was or anything. It nearly ruined me Junior Cert. *Normal People*, the Roscrea edition. I'd go home and listen to pop-punk, making every song about her. Wow, I was some saddo.

Scraps

JS: Whenever we talk about school, someone inevitably asks, 'Were there fights in your school?' In Roscrea? Are ya joking? Does Brian Cody wear a hat? There were loads of fights, but they always came in a cluster. If there was a fight on Monday, you could be sure there'd be four or five more by Wednesday. Lads would see a scrap and they'd get hyped up and want a bit of the limelight themselves: 'I'd love that, everyone shouting at me.'

Students would fight over anything. I once saw two lads fight over which team was better, Liverpool or Man United. I saw two girls fighting one day, and holy God they beat the dirt out of each other. There's a village in Laois called Camross, and for years they've had a rivalry with Roscrea. This occasionally spilled over into school, where lads from both places attended. One time Camross fought Roscrea for a whole week every lunchtime for no apparent reason, probably just boredom. It was like Royal Rumble every lunch, and then they'd all have to go back into class with each other.

Thankfully I was never in a proper fight after school. Years ago I got a beating off a really small lad because I wouldn't fight back. Then I got a bit of advice from an older cousin. He said, 'You're gonna have to stand up for yourself.' The next time a lad picked on me was in first year of secondary school and, well, I went all out to come across hard as nails. Acting hard was more important than being hard. It was all about making noise and throwing shapes. I'd shout and shadow-box like I knew what I was doing, but in reality if anyone had actually come at me, I'd probably have run home to Mammy. But that day in first year, I threw a few shapes and a few jabs and the rumour went out that Johnny Mc was hard as nails. The way I told it, I nearly killed your man.

Teachers

JS: I was lucky to have had some great teachers during my six years in San Quentin . . . sorry, I mean Coláiste Phobal Ros Cré. When we got a new woodwork teacher, he quickly realized that all the tools in our classroom were shite. Pure useless. He asked the principal for funds to buy some new tools and materials, which would have been a massive help to everyone involved, but it was a no go. Instead he printed off sponsorship cards and gave them to every student. We were to collect money for a sponsored walk up the Slieve Bloom Mountains. It was genius on the teacher's behalf. It raised enough money to buy new saws, chisels, the works. Singlehandedly he must have raised about €10,000. But we never did the walk. I'd say he had no intention of dragging a bunch of teenagers up a mountain. Fifteen years later and I still haven't been up the Slieve Bloom Mountains.

JB: *There was a rumour going around that our English teacher once had a breakdown in class and crouched under the table shouting, 'The Germans are coming!' Lads used to push her buttons in class, hoping to get a glimpse of her World War II flashbacks for themselves. Looking back now, I never did meet anyone who actually witnessed it and it sounds pretty far-fetched. A friend's older sister heard she once had a bottle of vodka in her car, so of course we all assumed she was an alcoholic. She had probably just done the shopping or was going somewhere after school, but these possibilities didn't occur to us back then.*

JS: There must be a trend with English teachers

because we had one who knew *Macbeth* off by heart. All of it. Line by line. He'd sit at the top of class with his hand over his eyes. He didn't even have a copy of the book. He just knew it. Someone would be reading and if they messed up a line, he'd correct them without moving. I swear he taught us for three years and never opened his eyes. He taught my mother too. She said he was the exact same back then. I'd say he must have invented school. He must be the only man to teach for forty years without ever opening his eyes.

JB: *There was one teacher in his sixties with a big white beard and a bit of timber around the mid-section. Danny Greene, or Mr Greene to us. He taught history, all from memory. He looked like he could have been around to meet the Normans. The big wild head on him, I'd say he was mates with the Vikings. He never used books or took notes. One time, upon hearing a distinctively droll comment from one of our classmates, Mr Greene ordered him up to the principal's office. As our classmate was leaving the room, he turned around and said, 'Ho, ho, ho, Danny.' We roared laughing, but Mr Greene never accepted that he had the head of Santa Claus. I think your man got suspended. I suppose you can't be calling teachers by their first names, or insinuate that they love coming down people's chimneys.*

JS: One teacher I had was a bit annoying. He had mad sideburns. Well, actually, what was weird was that he had no sideburns at all. It looked like he shaved them off completely. That bothered me as a fifteen-year-old and it still bothers me now. Why do that? He always carried an old beat-up Ballygowan bottle, too. The lads in our class were always trying to get one over on him, and one day they got their chance when he got up and left class for a moment. The boys pierced his beloved Ballygowan bottle with a thumbtack several times. When he went to take a drink, it squirted all over him. We all tried to contain the giggling. He was trying to control our excitement: 'It's only a dribble, it's only a dribble.' There were lads nearly passing out from laughter. Jaysus he was wet enough, but he was hell-bent on drinking out of the bottle and getting another few years out of it. The following week, he walked into class and announced, 'An incident happened here last week, and after closer inspection, it appears my water bottle had been sabotaged. The culprit can visit me after class.' We never told him, but it was Joe Carroll. Joe, you owe that man a plastic bottle.

My favourite part of the school week was PE. Ninety minutes of running around, and then you put on your shirt and go to double Irish, the sweat still pumping out of you. Certainly not the most hygienic set-up. Our PE teacher used to join in and play soccer with us. We'd spend the whole class trying to tackle him. He was a tough bastard, though. He'd be trash-talking us and all. He was good, too, in fairness, even though he was around fifty. During one game, my classmate Anthony, who was a big rugby lad, tried to mash the teacher against the fence, but the teacher side-stepped him and ran off with the ball, while Anto hopped off the fence.

For a while we had a PE teacher on placement – David Young from Toomevara. He was hurling for Tipperary at the time, and won an All-Ireland in 2010. He managed our school's senior hurling team.

Sometimes he'd join in the training sessions. He'd stand in full-back with no helmet on and I'd have to mark him, and he playing full-back for Tipp at the time. I wanted to mark some harmless lad from Moneygall and score 1–6, not inter-county Dave with quads like a bullock. One time a ball broke and I went to flick it away, and I accidentally caught him with the hurl right across the nose. He instantly dropped the ball and hurley and turned around as if he was ready to scrap. I was petrified. Another teacher shouted in from the sideline, 'OK, David, that'll do.' It was instinct for him. I thought he was going to kill me. He decided not to murder me, but he gave me a look to suggest that if we met in club hurling he might not be so forgiving. The next ball that came in, I just let him have it.

Really, though, the best thing about PE was the fact that there was no homework. Also, it was a chance to settle scores. Boys would be killing each other during indoor soccer. Some schools did gymnastics, Olympic handball and a whole range of exotic sports; our teacher said, 'Pick two teams,' and that was it – ninety minutes of indoor soccer every week for six years.

We do have massive respect for teachers and the job they do. To any teachers reading this, we salute you. Ye have some patience. A lot of teachers listen to our podcast, so it was no surprise that after we put out a call for tales about when teaching went wrong we got some crackers in. We kept the senders anonymous so they wouldn't lose their job, their pension and four months' holidays a year. To be fair, it doesn't sound that bad a job. Here are some of our favourites:

Hi Johnnies,

I have a story relating to your recent episode where you discussed feckin' up at work.

I started my first proper teaching job at twenty-one and had to move to the UK at the time because of the recession. Needless to say, as sound as the English were, they were minus craic, and failed to see the funny side of any situation, which didn't bode well for me, as my friends often referred to me as the real-life version of An Idiot Abroad.

As most people do, I embellished my skill set for the interview and told a little white lie. I said that I could coach football, having never played, watched, spoken about or had any prior knowledge of the sport. I'm just one of those lads who was never into sport!

A few months had passed and I thought I had got away with it, as I had become involved in other extracurricular activities across the school. Then, one day, the PE teacher came to me and said, 'I heard you're interested in coaching Year 10 football.' And me, a young lad, desperate to make a decent impression at the school, said, 'Yeah, sure. I love football, I'd be happy to help.'

Now, needless to say, I was shitting myself. I frantically watched some YouTube videos explaining the basics of the sport, and even looked up some players' names and recent match scores to be prepared for any small talk people tried to make.

Eventually, the day of the match came. It was an away game so we had to drive almost two hours to another school in the freezing cold. As we hopped off the bus, the PE teacher said to me, 'Do the line, will you?'

'No bother,' says I.

I went over to this group of boys who must have been fifteen or sixteen years old and said, 'Right lads, everybody run in a line.' In their confusion they replied, 'Why, sir?' I panicked and said, 'Don't be answering back, lads. Now go run in a line.' So off these lads went running in a line. I thought I was doing a great job. Maybe football ran in my veins and all along I could have been great at this sport. The midlands' answer to Roy Keane.

The bubble eventually burst when the PE teacher came over to me and said, 'Why the fuck are they running in a line?' All of a sudden, it was panic stations. All of the lads huddled around and tried to explain to me what 'doing the lines' meant. I was very confused when I was handed a flag and told, 'Wave this when it's offside.' But what was this thing called offside? I had never looked this up on YouTube. Surely it can't be that hard to understand?

So there I was, twenty-one, in my shirt and tie, standing on the side of a football pitch with no fucking notion of what I was doing, screaming 'OFFSIDE' at random times throughout the match, with a twelve-year-old who was brought to carry equipment trying to explain to me what the offside rule actually was, and me not being able to comprehend the feckin' concept in the slightest.

The PE teacher eventually made me come off the pitch as I kept calling offside when it wasn't. And I was at the wrong end of the pitch. And I was waving for the wrong team. And it was blatantly clear that I hadn't a fucking notion what I was doing.

After the match I was told that I had brought the school into disrepute. I didn't know what to say except football is different in Ireland. We do different things like use our hands and not wave flags. The ball is a bit different too, like! To this day I still don't know if any of this is true, but the young lads I taught never let me forget it. In class, even though they might not have passed their Christmas tests, they always reminded me that they still knew the right way to kick a ball around a pitch. I never lied on my CV ever again.

Unrelated but also worth mentioning, just to give you an idea of the impression I left in that school before I left to return home to Ireland. The department I was in had a trolley of about thirty laptops that we shared. All you had to do was wheel them into your classroom and plug them in to charge. One day, in my last month at the school, I pulled the trolley of laptops out from the wall too hard and ended up breaking the lead at the back of the trolley. I was so scared, as I had already fucked up so much at this school and really wanted to leave with a decent reference.

So I did the only thing I could think of and put the two parts of the lead that had broken away from one another back together and let it be somebody else's problem.

What I didn't take into consideration was that one end of the lead was still plugged into the wall, so when I joined them together sparks flew, there was a huge bang and it started a small fire. All thirty laptops that were plugged into the charging ports in the trolley had experienced a huge jolt of electricity that blew the battery in most of them.

I could go on forever about all the different times I fecked up in that school and probably every school I've been in since, but I know ye haven't all day.

Anyway, loving the podcast and looking forward to seeing you both at the Marquee in Cork!

All the best,

An idiot abroad!

* * *

Well, lads,

As ye were on the topic of teachers last week, I've a hilarious/career-ending story for ye.

One of the lads from home is a primary teacher. One day two teachers in his school decided to send a few notes to each other via students from their class. They were having a right laugh until one of the students actually stopped to read one of the notes being passed along. The note read, 'This is my ugliest student. Send me yours.' The student didn't see the funny side of it anyway and went to the principal. Fairly sure the two lads were sent packing. Not the way you'd want to go out.

Anon

Sport

JB: *Sport was a big part of school in Cahir, and some of my fondest memories are sport-related. At one stage our school started a rugby team. Munster were going well and rugby was taking off. The problem was that most lads were flat out with GAA or soccer. We played rugby once for PE and a few boys got rightly smashed up. So after an eye-gouge or two, a bloody nose and getting covered in muck, most of the GAA lads decided kicking points was more glamorous, and they retired from the oval ball. The squad was then made up of guys who didn't play GAA or soccer, which means lads who weren't big into sport. I'm not knocking you, lads, but that first school rugby team was some bunch of sod-busters – 90 per cent tractor men who had never seen a hamstring stretch before. I can tell you one thing, though, there would be no easy tries conceded. Never was a tougher, more agricultural bunch of sixteen-year-old auld fellas thrown together. These were fellas who ran with their legs completely straight and warmed up by discussing milk quotas. They had fed calves and mucked out sheds before going to primary school. Try telling them to roll away after a tackle! There was one lad who actually played for a rugby club in the second row. For our team, he was taking kicks, throwing line-outs, and he was nearly catching them too. The* *team came back from their first match, and he had scored everything – two tries, conversions, drop goals, penalties. He even won the toss. All from the second row. That was sixth year. It took them years to recover after he left the school.*

JS: I gave the rugby a shot too. My history teacher said to me one day, 'Big man like you, you could probably play rugby.' This history teacher happened to be Seamus Dennison, who played in the famous Munster win over the All Blacks and is renowned for a tackle in that game that nearly broke some All Black in half. So I wasn't going to argue with him when he suggested I give rugby a go.

I showed up to my first training session and obviously I was class at it. I just kept taking drop goals, and they kept going over, about five in a row. Unbelievable. They played me in the second row for my first match. I was like, 'Can I not be the kicker?' They said I didn't have the pace. I ignored that, and every time I got the ball, I kicked it. They were good kicks, but it was just unorthodox for a prop to be kicking. Then I tackled a South African lad who played for the Roscrea boarding school and he poked me in the eye. After the game my eye was all bloodshot and I thought, *Well, that's it. I'm not playing that again.* I retired, but have no doubt, I'd probably have played for Munster if I had stuck at it.

We got hammered in that game. Our hooker was shouting these calls at the line-out like, 'Black Jack, two, four,' and I was confused, wondering what the fuck he was talking about. I hadn't a clue. I just picked up some random fucker on my team. It didn't help that I had no idea of the rules. If I saw the ball, I'd just go grab it. I could've been a mile offside. It also turned out that the reason our coach didn't want me to kick it was because we weren't able to do line-outs. See, I never went to the lunchtime training where they ran the plays. I only went to matches to get a day off school. The jerseys weren't even nice either. Rugby just wasn't my style in more ways than one.

Getting good results in your Leaving Cert was a big deal in my school but there was one thing that was more important than that to me and a lot of the lads – hurling. It was my main subject throughout school and all of us Roscrea lads tried to make sure we got on the starting team when championship came around. You didn't want some lad from Laois or Offaly taking your friend's place. I'd be marking my buddy Robert and I'd say, 'Hey, let me score this one and then you clear the next one.' By the end of the training session, I'd have six points and he'd have a few inspirational clearances. The other forwards would be fighting to the death against some corner back from the bog. Always look after your friends.

JB: *Some schools are great for sport. When Tipp won an All-Ireland, I went to visit a few schools with the team, and young lads would be mad to hear the Tipp song. I came from a school where you weren't allowed to hurl on the grass at lunch because someone would get hurt or something (there were fellas breaking each other's legs in our prison-rules soccer, but anyway). I'll never forget the sight of an entire school pucking fifty sliotars in among teachers' cars in the car park of a north*

Tipperary secondary school. It was like a beehive - boys, girls, sliotars, hurls - a beautiful sight.

I asked, 'Do they break many windows?'

The principal replied, 'Ah, a few, but sure they can be replaced.'

Unreal. Sport is an integral part of school life and we hope it stays that way.

Style

JS: Looking cool was something I attempted to pull off throughout my schooldays. For around seven years I constantly smelled of Lynx Africa. I'd say I even sweated Lynx Africa. I applied so much that the mother needed a gas mask in the car on the way to school. People definitely smelt me before they saw me. In fifth year I discovered aftershave. Burberry Brit, to be precise. My mother got it for me one Christmas and I put it on every day going to school. Pure Macaulay Culkin in *Home Alone* job. Did the girls like it? The results were inconclusive.

The next step of my ultracool look was Brylcreem Wet Look Gel. This was hair gel that made you look like you were constantly in a rain shower. I couldn't get enough in my hair. It was caked in it. If you're looking for a reference point, think Simon from *The Inbetweeners*, but worse. Looking back, I think it was all to impress women. I don't know who decided the wet look gel looked cool, but I got the memo, big time. There were times it went wrong - you'd put in too much gel and have to wash it out and reapply. Some mornings I'd skip breakfast to get it right. The hair was more important than a mouldy bowl of cornflakes. In sixth year I had a blond Mohican streak going diagonally across my head, like a rundown badger. That look was hard to style. Honestly, I could be half an hour doing my hair for school. And I have no regrets.

It was compulsory that we all wore the full uniform, but I had a hurling jacket that said MUNSTER CHAMPIONS on it that I'd won in third year. I'm fairly sure I was still wearing it in sixth year. It was average enough, cheap material, but I wore it because it made me feel like the high school American football players you see on TV shows. It was the closest I could get.

The school uniform was a disaster. If the big hairy jumper got wet, you'd instantly die with the weight of it. But it was the pants I had the real issue with. I was chunky but funky. The pants weren't designed for someone with an arse like Shakira and thighs like Hulk Hogan. One day, bending down to pick up my schoolbag, I split my trousers. So as not to reveal my boxers, I tied my jumper around my waist and asked the principal if I could ring my mother to drop me down a new pair. He said, 'Aren't you grand the way you are?' I then made the fatal mistake of telling the boys about my mishap. They ripped the jumper off me, and there was my arse hanging out. This became a regular occurrence. In six years of school, I must have ripped twenty pairs of pants. My poor mother nearly had to remortgage the house. 'My poor Jonathan,' she'd say, and I eighteen stone in fifth year. Nothing poor about it.

I also invented Dubarry shoes. Well, *invented* is a bit strong, but I was the first in our school to wear them. You'd pull any trick to avoid wearing the old Wrangler black shoes, which were in no way comfortable and looked like you were wearing actual shoeboxes on your feet. I'd seen lads in Thurles and Nenagh wearing Dubes, as they were called, at the school matches, and I made it my mission to introduce Dubarry shoes to Roscrea. When lads first saw them, they laughed and said, 'Ah, lad, you're like an auld lad with the shoe.' The girls liked them, though, and one day I was talking to a few female classmates about them and they started showing me how to tie the laces in different, funky ways. Three months later every fella was wearing them.

JB: *It must be tough being a teenager now, posting pictures on social media all done up. When we were in school, if a girl was showing a bit of knee, you'd be dreaming about it for weeks. Make-up wasn't allowed, and you could spot the girls wearing fake tan a mile away because they looked like a roast turkey leg. Make-up tutorials weren't a big thing like they are now.*

I had long hair in school, and to be fair it seemed quite impractical until the day I was cast in the lead role of Jesus Christ Superstar, *our school musical. My mate Mick had long hair too, so he was Pontius Pilate. Two more mates signed up on the premise that they could play the guards who whipped Jesus (me). Neither of them were into singing; I think they just wanted to bate me. We assembled the roughest twelve apostles in history. If these lads had been around back in the day, the Romans would have been stabbed before they got near our Lord, and their wallets gone as well. The lad playing Peter actually wore a System of a Down (the heavy metal band) T-shirt on stage every night. He didn't give a shit.*

Fun fact: King Herod was played by Irish international rugby player Tommy O'Donnell. He wasn't as big back then.

To any young people reading, I'd highly recommend some extra activities while in school. The musical was a great experience, and because I was playing the lead role, they couldn't suspend me when the principal caught me in the girls' toilets with Mary Magdalene. Also, they let us hang out in the music room, and the boys flaked everything that wasn't nailed down: drum sticks, drum stools, a trumpet. They even stole the strings off the bass guitar. A week later I saw two young lads kicking the trumpet around a local housing estate. I don't think I was expecting a ska-punk movement to spring up in south Tipperary, but I thought they'd find better use for it than that. Their father said to me, 'Ah sure, the auld music keeps them outta trouble.' Amen.

Subjects

JS: One of the big decisions you have to make in school is what subjects you're going to study. This can have an impact on what job you end up doing, but that never entered my mind. For example, I chose home economics over woodwork and metalwork. I didn't like dust or getting dirty, so home ec' seemed the logical choice. In my Leaving Cert year there were forty-two students taking the subject: forty-one girls and me. Being the only lad in class certainly didn't hurt. When I did it for the Junior Cert, there was one other fella. He must have been there by accident because on the first day, he put his pencil case in the microwave and left it to cook for twelve minutes, until it blew up.

At first he said, 'Miss, that wasn't me.'

The teacher said, 'But it's your pencil case.'

He said, 'It's not.'

She asked, 'Well, where's yours?'

'I don't have one.'

'Your name's written on it.'

'Well, I didn't think it'd blow up.'

He eventually got thrown out, and I think he was secretly delighted.

Deciding what subjects to do and what career path you want to go down is tough. I still don't know what I want to do now, let alone back when I was sixteen. When I went to meet the career guidance counsellor, I told her I was going to play for Liverpool. She said, 'You're sixteen and you've had a knee operation.' I was also fairly overweight at the time, which didn't help my case. I was hoping one day I'd be playing for my local club, Killavilla, and a scout would see me and say, 'He'll slot in fairly nicely up front with Milan Baroš.' The guidance counsellor made me take an aptitude test on the computer and it said I should be a gardener. I nearly put the computer through the wall. 'Twas playing on the grass I wanted to be, not mowing it. If I had told her I wanted to be a comedian, author, podcaster and TV presenter, she'd have laughed me out of it for saying that too. You have to always keep dreaming. You never know.

JB: *My parents suggested I drop history, as I was fairly dyslexic and it had a lot of names and dates. Sure, I'd never remember them all. I took up art in fifth year because I'd heard it was great craic and my mate Grinder was doing it. There was another lad in class who* *was gifted at art, drawing, painting, charcoal, anything. His favourite part of the class was ceramics. At the time, there was an old man around the town who played fiddle and busked at tourists, and our mate just made clay models of your man every day. Different colours, different sizes. He kept at it even though the teacher pleaded with him to make better use of his considerable talents and at least try to pass the exams. Nah, more clay fiddle-players every day. One day he made a bus for the tourists and all. He's a professional painter now, of pictures I mean, not houses. I follow him on Instagram and haven't seen any fiddlers in a while, so the joke must have eventually gone flat.*

JS: I did German for my Leaving Cert for one simple reason: to go on a school trip to Germany. My friend Chris, who was a year above me, was going with all the lads, so there was no way I was missing that. I basically did two years of torture so I could spend four days in a shit hostel in Cologne. We went on a boat down the Rhine and saw a hawk show. I hate birds, by the way. A lad from Camross nearly got killed by a big hawk. The bird trainer put a bit of food on his head and the bird was to swoop down and snatch it, but I'd say your man hadn't brushed his hair in ten years, and this hawk nearly pulled the head off him. Somehow I managed to pass honours German for my Leaving. The oral saved me. It turns out I can even talk shit in German.

I blame failing biology for messing up my Leaving Cert, but three times a week I was GAA training in Thurles, and the other evenings, well, I'd find something better to do than study anyway. It didn't do me any harm. Thankfully everything worked out in the end. But trust us, school days are most definitely the best days of your life.

THE DEBS

JS: Let's take it from the top. It was 2009. I was at my peak – county minor. My school was in an All-Ireland final on the telly. I felt like I was John Travolta in *Grease*, without the white socks. I was on top of the world.

The summer before, I had been at the Gaeltacht, where I met a girl from south Tipperary who I fancied. But she was going out with a fella, so it was a no go, but we kept in contact after. When I was looking for a debs date, she was my first port of call. I had exhausted all options in Roscrea – it's a small town. I asked her and she said ya. I asked my mother if she could stay at our house, because it's a bit of a spin. My mother said no bother – all good. Then the plan ran into difficulty, choppy waters if you will.

I was also pursuing a girl from Templemore at the same time, so I was desperate to get an invite to the Templemore debs because she'd be there. It'd be a chance for me to show her my moves on the dance floor, the old John Travolta hand jive. Then word got to me that a female friend of mine from Templemore had said, 'If he brings me to his debs, I'll bring him to the Templemore debs.' It seemed like an *I'll scratch your back and you scratch mine* set-up, and we'd both get the shift from the debs. It was a win-win situation. Now, that reads like we were both in on the plan, but to be honest, only I was in on the plan. I think she fancied me, and I told her I had a few friends in her school who I wanted to have pints with.

So I did what any eighteen-year-old fella would do – I followed my willie. I didn't use my brain to think; that would be too much like hard work. I agreed to the Templemore home-and-away match. This meant I had to give the dummy hand pass to the south Tipp girl, who at this stage had told her friends and parents about the debs and had bought an expensive dress. I know it was a dick move but it all worked out – I'll tell you about that later. At the time she was heartbroken, though, and everyone in south Tipp thought I was a prick (nothing new there, so), probably still do to this day.

So the Templemore debs rolled around. I went into Moran's Menswear in Roscrea and got myself a nice suit. I thought, *Wow, I look sharp!* But unfortunately the lads in Templemore weren't thinking along the same lines as me when it came to fashion. I arrived at the Templemore Arms Hotel to the sight of 200 lads in black suits with black dickie bows and black shoes. I flounced in the door in a pinstripe suit with a cream, diamond-encrusted waistcoat and a matching cream cravat. A fucking cravat! Who wears a cravat to a debs? What was I thinking? If you think that was a bad start, things were about to get a whole lot worse. To this day I think this is the most embarrassed I've ever been.

My mate Willie was at the debs, and he whispered to me, 'What the hell are you wearing?'

I said, 'Jaysus, lad, you could have given me the heads up!'

He said, 'Ah ya, they'd be fairly traditional around here.'

I said, 'It's only ten minutes out the road, for God's sake. How can things be so different?'

Back home in Roscrea they were wearing white suits and sovereign rings, like rougher versions of Snoop Dogg. How can two towns be so different? A Roscrea debs was the closest thing I'd seen to Paris fashion week. I'd say my cravat was the talk of Templemore for weeks.

Anyway, we headed into the ballroom and took our seats. I was only just sat down when over came the one I actually fancied.

'Well, how are you?' she says.

I was just thinking, *Wow, she is gorgeous. This is great.* But I played it cool: 'Not too bad. Yourself?'

Then I watched as she put her arm around her new boyfriend, who it turned out was a county hurler. How could I compete with that?

My mood instantly changed. I met a fella I knew from around there and decided it was time to get drunk and nurse my crushed heart. He introduced me to 'Purple Haze'. Now, this was not the song made famous by Jimi Hendrix or some fella called Hayes, but the three colours of Aftershock mixed together and downed in one shot. Sounds OK? It's not. It's horrific. But we had another Purple Haze between every course: starter, Purple Haze, vol-au-vent, Purple Haze, spuds, meat . . . Jesus, by the time they came around with the tea and coffee, I was rotten drunk. Then just as the band were setting up, I got this feeling like the room was spinning (seven shots of Purple Haze tend to do that to a fella).

I went and sat down in the toilets. Man, I was feeling tired at that stage. Then BANG! Someone kicked the door in. It was a bouncer asking, 'Are you all right?' I said, 'I was until you kicked the door off me head.' My friend Willie picked me up off the toilet. I put my arm around him and he helped me out of the jacks as if I was some hurler who'd done his knee in in an All-Ireland final in Croker and needed to be helped off the field. He walked me out to the ballroom but there was no one there. It turned out I went to the toilet at 9.15 p.m. and it was now 2.45 a.m. I had slept in the toilet for the entire night.

When I went outside, I was reunited with my date, who had phoned my mother. Not ideal. My date put me into the back of the mother's car and she hopped in as well and we gave her a lift home. My mam was as nice as pie, just saying sorry on my behalf. Then for the entire drive from my date's house in Barnane to Roscrea, the mother told me what a disgrace I was. I did not need her to tell me. I knew. I would just like to take this opportunity to apologize to Carol Hasset, I was a terrible date. My mam also put the boot in and added, 'I told you no one would be wearing cravats, you clown.' Another blow to contend with the next morning as I nursed the hangover from hell.

Three weeks later, it was my turn to take Carol to the return leg, my debs in Roscrea, as agreed. I made sure I was the perfect gentleman, danced with her all night and filled her full of vodka and white. This time I wore a grey suit, like Leonardo DiCaprio in *The Wolf of Wall Street*, and fitted right in. That was all the rage in Roscrea at the time. I've never seen so many diamond earrings in one place, and I'm not talking about the girls. I'd say Carol didn't know what to make of the place. Did she have a good night? You'd have to ask her. She hasn't really spoken much to me since.

JB: *There are different trends from school to school. Apparently everyone in Fermoy got a limo. In Cahir we got a fifty-two-seater bus.*

JS: In 2008 everyone in Roscrea wore a cravat.

JB: *Back in my day we rented suits. At my debs it was all black suits and dickie bows. Skinny-legged trousers hadn't been invented yet.*

I was due to start my apprenticeship the day after my debs. I said, 'Ah here, can we push it back a bit?' So I started a day later. I was sitting on a milk crate beside the van drinking tay, attempting to get to know my new co-workers, when who stumbled past only one of my former classmates. He was still in his rented suit, as he had kept partying after the debs, on to a house party and then into day two. He was looking like a mobster after fist-fighting a man to death and I had to let on I didn't know him that well. I hope he got his deposit back.

In Dublin many debs nights ended with a trip to the Leisureplex because some of them were open twenty-four-hours. A bit of air hockey and shooting each other with lasers, just in case the suits had fooled anyone into thinking that they were adults. I tell ya, you wouldn't hang around Clonmel all night; you'd die of exposure or end up in a gang.

The main shock at the debs was seeing girls from your class done up. Wow, where did you get that bra, and also those things in the bra? They're like tracker beams.

Seventeen-year-old lads are helpless against their powers. Several lads got a slap in the face for staring too hard. 'Jaysus, sorry, Tracey. I wouldn't have been so mean to you in school if I knew you had big jugs.' Ah, the innocence of youth. At some stage in your twenties you realize this is totally inappropriate. There's a scene in Normal People where Connell stares at a painting for six hours. Give a teenager a few pints and boobs have the same effect.

One question I'd love to know the answer to is: Why are the photos from the debs so shiny? Everyone looks like porcelain dolls.

JS: Ours were taken by the school caretaker. They didn't even bother to get a professional. The man who a few hours previously had been mopping out the jacks was now seemingly a qualified photographer.

JB: And who can forget the debs pose, when the photographer directs you to put your hand on your date's shoulder in the exact same pose as the other 200 couples?

Another regular occurrence in the lead-up to the debs is that there's always someone accused of stealing money from the kitty. It happened in our year. I've no idea if it was true but your man had to leave town anyway.

Nowadays there are often awards at the debs. Not for prom queen like in America, but the stuff that really matters like Biggest Ride or Most Likely to Drop out of College. A girl will take the mic and scream the name of her friends as they win all the awards. She's rehearsing for when she is a county councillor in ten years' time and loves every minute she gets in the spotlight.

We made one appearance at a debs when we were starting out as The 2 Johnnies. We thought it could be a potential earner for us as we hadn't started gigging yet. They handed us a giant confetti cannon and Smacks was to set it off when the beat dropped in some random dance song. We were thinking about what an entrance we'd make. The DJ announced, 'Are ye ready for the best part of the night?' slowly building up to when the massive beat was going to kick in. The organizer handed over the cannon to Smacks, and just as the DJ gave the crowd another 'Are ye ready?' – BANG! Smacks set the yoke off thirty seconds too early, confetti everywhere. Total professionals. We never did another debs. We couldn't even get that much right.

Students are under a lot of pressure to find a date, and for months beforehand every Tom, Dick and Harry is asking, 'Who are you bringing to the debs?' I think going 'stag' is always an option if you don't have a date. Two lads in my school went together for the craic. They didn't even wear suits. One of them was locked and fell asleep on the bus. He spent the whole debs night parked outside the hotel, conked out. He said he had no regrets.

JS: I ran into a problem because I did transition year, and many of my friends were a year ahead of me. The debs was all they were talking about. It was non-stop debs, debs, debs, suits, dates, oh it's going to be some craic, and I just thought, *I'm not having this. I'm getting to that debs one way or another.* It was time to come up with a plan. It didn't take me long. One Saturday when I was working in Lifestyle Sports, this girl comes in. She was in my friend Chris's year. I kind of half-knew her.

She was friends with my cousin, you know that kind of way. Anyway, she was browsing the runners and I was on her like Brian Cody on to a referee. First, I kept it professional, asking her if there was anything I could get her.

She said, 'Have ya these in a size 5?'

I said, 'Have you a date for the debs?'

She was a bit taken aback. Anyway, I got her the shoes and as she was trying them on, we got talking about the debs. She said she had asked a fella but he wasn't much craic, so I laid my cards on the table.

I said, 'Hey, I'll go with ya. I'm some craic and I'll give ya 20 per cent off the shoes.'

She said she'd keep me in mind, but in my mind it was a great start. At least the seed was planted. I like to think it was my personality and go-get-'em attitude and not the staff discount that swung it. So I texted my cousin who was friends with her to get her number. Then I texted her, saying, 'Well, how are the runners?' Classic. After a week or two of texting and meeting up once (we may have shifted), she asked me to go to the debs.

This is about a month out from the debs. The best part of it all was being able to tell Chris I was going to the debs. Ya see, I was only in fifth year, so I was breaking new ground and to me this was class. She even agreed to sit at the table with all my friends. In fairness to her, she bucked the trend. Normally it was girls taking older lads who drove souped-up Starlets, Honda Civics or pimped Opel Corsas, but she'd taken a chance on me and I was going to pay her back. I went all out in the lead-up. I got my mother to buy aftershave, a corsage (which is a flower that women traditionally wear on their wrist, for no apparent reason – as far as I'm concerned they're a waste of money), flowers for her mother, whiskey for her father. Right job. I had to get my mother to fund this splurge as I had lost the job in Lifestyle Sports by this time, which had nothing to do with abusing the staff discount.

So debs day finally came. Myself, Chris and our mate Shane went for one pint to settle the nerves at lunchtime while picking up the flowers our mothers had ordered on our behalf. Chris and I headed home after one drink to start our beauty regime of dangerous amounts of Brylcreem, leaving Shane in the pub. When I passed his date's house later on, he was in the front garden getting photos. He was cross-eyed and could barely stand up. He'd overdone it and had to put up with his date's mam calling him a disgrace as he stumbled around her garden attempting to pose for photographs. He was buried.

When I was leaving my house, all the neighbours were out in force, waving me off like I was going to war, never to be seen again. I was only going to Racket Hall, which was two miles away. After the long goodbye, we picked up my date at her house, and this was when my mother went into overdrive. She was taking photos from every angle, lying on the ground and all. I had to stop her climbing a tree at one stage to 'get a good photo'. She must have taken a million photos and the sweat was beading out of me. I could have done with a second shirt.

Eventually we got to the debs. This was going to be a great night – all of us at one table, thinking we were the cast of *American Pie*. Then a lad on the soccer team got the wrong change from the barman and tried to hop the counter to correct the error. He knocked over six taps and the alcohol sprayed everywhere. The hotel staff turned on the lights and stopped the music.

'Everybody out!'

So that was a premature end to the night. We got a shuttle bus back to Roscrea. Two hundred girls in ballgowns and lads looking like something out of *The Sopranos* all milled into Supermac's for a sing-song. Whispers of a house party started going around, but there was none to be found. Before I knew it, I was at home talking shit to my mother.

What a night. I'd say it was the handiest few quid John Gibbons ever got. They had booked him to DJ and he'd only done about twenty minutes before we got kicked out. All that build-up for nothing. My date for the night must still think I'm sound, because she has tickets to come see us when we play in Vancouver.

JB: *Thankfully, unlike Smacks, I wasn't lingering around debs like a bad smell. I only went to my own one. But that doesn't mean I haven't experienced my fair share of debs. When I was in a cover band, I played a bunch of them. A hotel where we regularly played recommended us because we were going down well at weddings. Unfortunately the debs didn't pay as well as weddings, but it was a mid-week gig, so happy days.*

It was a big hotel, and one time there were only seventy people at the debs, so it was hard to fill the dance floor. We weren't sure what they wanted but we tried our pub setlist: The Killers, Kings of Leon, etc. Not much of a reaction. Eventually a girl came up and, in a tremendously strong Limerick accent, shouted, 'Do you know any Kesha?' Kesha is an American singer/rapper whose breakthrough was a duet with Flo Rida. Christ, there were four lads in our band, all with long hair and beards; the boys thought Kesha was something you smoked.

Not to discriminate, but it was clear what kind of school it was by their song requests. A good school with an active music department would have sixteen-year-olds asking for James Brown and Queen. I'll put it this way, if they requested Tinchy Stryder, I'd be double-locking the van.

When we first started playing at debs it was great craic. We were about twenty, rocking on in our matching black and white suits, but by our twenty-seventh or twenty-eighth one, we started to feel it wasn't so cool for us to be impressing eighteen-year-old young wans, and we went back to impressing auld wans at weddings.

I've never seen anything too crazy at these debs, apart from the usual 'I can't believe that bitch has the same dress as me' situations, and girls assuring their friend that 'he's only a prick and you're too good for him'.

Along with this carry-on, there's always glass on the floor, and the girls are in their bare feet because they've never worn high heels before. The main job of a band at a debs is to constantly remind everyone not to bring drinks onto the dance floor and to put their shoes back on. God, I've had hotel managers come close to a breakdown at the side of the stage, screaming, 'Why don't they wear shoes? Why?'

There can be too much drink taken and damage is

done from time to time. Pulling a sink off the bathroom wall is not a good idea. Get a job in construction and someday you'll be paid to do that. In the meantime, take your frustration out on the football pitch and not on defenceless hotel bathrooms. Don't let it get out of hand like these ones did:

- In 2009, the *Mayo News* reported that students at a debs after-party (held in 2008) caused €8,000 worth of damage to a cottage they had rented under false pretences.

- An article in the *Meath Chronicle* in 2009 described how attendees at a debs in Trim caused up to €3,000 in criminal damage and saw 'a number' of staff assaulted.

- In 2015 Joe.ie reported that two lads from a Dublin school ended up in Paris after their debs, having travelled through the night.

- A petition appeared on Change.org looking for signatures to support four boys who were being banned from going to their debs because they put a fish in five classrooms in their school. There was a bad smell but no one was hurt. The students of Coachford College, County Cork, gathered 2,800 signatures and the four boyos were allowed to attend. No fish were harmed at the debs.

JB: *Wicked carry-on altogether.*

JS: My final appearance at the debs was after I had left school. I was twenty. Too old to go to a debs? Yes, I agree. Having flunked out of college, I was now working in the bacon factory. I came home and the mother was being real nice to me. I knew there was something up.

I said, 'What's your story'?

She said, 'Ah, nothing. Next door rang. She wanted to know would you go to the debs with her daughter.'

I laughed and said, 'I'm a bit old for that now.'

She said, 'It's too late. I told her you would.'

I said, 'Well, you can un-tell her.'

Mam talked me around and offered to pay for everything. I had no choice in the matter.

A particular bugbear of mine with debs is fellas having to wear the same colour waistcoat and bow tie as the girl's dress. I was carrying a few pounds at the time and the lilac waistcoat wasn't doing anything for me. The worst of it, though, was at the table when all her friends started talking about what bright futures they had in front of them: 'Oh, I'm going to study journalism in UL', 'I'm doing medicine in Trinity', etc.

'What are you up to, Jonathan?' one of them asked me.

'I dropped out of college and work in the bacon factory,' I said.

I used to give out about the lads in Honda Civics but at least they had a car. I had nothing.

It all ended in Supermac's again, and this time there was a house party, but I didn't go. I told them all I had work in the morning in the factory. I didn't fancy having to explain my dropping out of college again. I hated the factory but I'd have hated that more. We are good neighbours.

And whatever happened to that girl from south

Tipperary who I dropped before my debs, I hear you ask? Well, next year she's marrying one of my best friends. All's well that ends well.

IRISH MAMMIES

JS: We were playing Portroe in the U14 North Tipperary Championship. I was doing well. I had scored a goal and a point in the first half, and then one of the Portroe mentors roared, 'Will someone mark that fat bastard!' So obviously I was upset, as any fourteen-year-old child would be. Now, to be fair, I was a fat bastard. I was carrying a few extra pounds, which was mainly down to an over-indulgence in Denny sausages. I was big-boned, stocky, whatever way you want to look at it. I told my cousin, who was watching the game from the sideline, what had happened. So at half-time we were in a huddle getting a team talk from our manager, when I looked over at the sideline and saw my cousin holding the fella who'd called me a fat bastard in a headlock, attempting to strangle him.

When your man started to get the better of my cousin, our manager told us, 'Don't mind all that. It's only handbags. Keep your head in the game.'

I said, 'I can't,' mainly due to the fact that my mother had just cleared an 8 ft fence and was sprinting onto the field. She jumped onto your man's back and put him in some sort of UFC sleeper hold. She was attempting some kind of yippee-ki-yay job. I didn't hear what was being said during the tangle but I'm sure it wasn't good. Eventually the referee and a few selectors broke it up and she returned to her place at the back of the stand. No one said a word; that was the done thing.

Back in those days women had their kids' backs – literally, in my case. During underage games I remember women shouting at referees, 'We're gonna ring Tipp FM in the morning about you!' All because he didn't give a free. The Roscrea mothers were kind of like Ultras at the time. English soccer clubs had the Green Street Elite and other groups of hooligans; we had the Roscrea Cougars – a bunch of disgruntled housewives.

I went out in the second half and scored 1-2. I think the fella marking me in the second half was more afraid of my mother than my football skills. He was probably thinking, *If I hurt this fella, his mother is gonna come down from the stand and choke me.* I half-slapped a fella while drop-shotting a ball. He fell down in pain and no one said a word. My mother was giving the death stare from the stand. When I give her a copy of this book, I'll have to cut out this chapter.

'Why are there only nine chapters?'

'I don't know. Talk to Penguin.'

JB: *There's a scene in* Goodfellas *where Joe Pesci's character has murdered a lad, and he, De Niro and Ray Liotta have a fella in the boot of the car. They pull in to Joe's mother's house to get a shovel, but she hears them. She comes out and says her son never calls and they have to come in for something to eat, because he's not eating right at all. Now, she probably has a fair idea what her son wants the shovel for – Joe Pesci's character isn't going digging spuds at four in the morning, dressed in a suit. He's a mobster. This doesn't bother her at all.*

The three boyos go in and have meatballs and pasta, and they eventually say they have to leave. The mother kisses Joe on the cheek and says he should call more often. He tips out the road and buries the body of some lad who insulted him. The mother is just happy her son visited. This is nothing to Irish mothers. Replace whacking mobsters with GAA training and drinking too much, and add in a few loads of washing and eventually minding the grandkids, and you're getting close. I rang my mam and said we were writing a chapter on Irish mammies.

'What should we say?' I asked.

My dad interjected, 'That they spoil their sons.'

JS: I think parenting has changed since we were young fellas. For example, Dozol seems to be gone off the market. That was like a massive dose of Calpol that was used to send you off to sleep. If you were born in the nineties, believe us when we tell you, if you acted the shite as a baby, you were sent to bed with a bottle of tea with a shot of Dozol in it.

Back then mothers used to just scare their kids into behaving better. Nowadays you can't do that. 'See that man? That man's gonna take you away. He's the boogie man. He's gonna take you away' was a common threat to young kids. That was fair scary. Like, what was he going to do with ya? He was just the butcher in SuperValu. Was he going to mince you? Were you going to be in Peggy Hanrahan's stew the next day? Who knows? We never messed around enough to find out.

JB: *When I worked in people's houses as a carpenter, mothers would often threaten their children with 'the* man': 'If you're bold, the man will take you away.' I played along, saying, 'Yep, I take the bold children.' If the kid was really annoying, I'd open the back door of the van and say to them, 'That's where they go.' Looking back now, I can see how the children were terrified, and I may have gone too far by holding up a hammer and saying, 'Finish your homework or it's into the van.' I guess the mothers didn't think I'd go that far into character. Jesus, this sounds awful. I think it was obvious I was only messing, as it didn't work in the tough housing estates. Young lads there were like feral cats. If you threatened them with the man, they'd say, 'Go on so!' and rob your tools. I swear to God a six-year-old robbed my measuring tape and threw it onto the motorway. Try and scare him with 'the man'.

JS: My mother used to say she was going to run away, and I'd be terrified, crying, 'Ah, Mam, please don't run away.'

She once said, 'That's it, I'm running away. I'm going to join the circus.' It would be fair funny if she did join the circus. Imagine going to Duffy's circus and there's my ma on the trapeze!

Every child in Ireland was threatened with the wooden spoon, but why the wooden spoon? It's not even the best kitchen utensil to hit someone with. Why not the rolling pin and give them a proper beating? Why not a spatula? Now that's a weapon.

I love my mam, no question about it, and as a near-thirty-year-old man I'm not afraid to say it. She also comes out with some great quotes from time to time. One of her favourites is, 'A son is a son until he marries his wife. A daughter is a daughter for the rest of her life.' What's this even supposed to mean? I reckon she means a son will be around until he finds a wife, and then she takes on the mammy role. It's seamless. The wife irons my clothes, cuts my toenails (yes, my mother used to cut my toenails. So what? It's a tricky job and super sore if you cut them down too far), keeps me warm, minds me when I'm sick. After the wife replaces the mammy, the son isn't around as much, while the daughter will be at the house most days, drinking tea and giving out about her husband. If the son gives out about his wife, the mother will say, 'Aw, I knew it. I always said she was a bitch.' In fact a son can't go to his mammy and give out about his wife, as the mother would go down and stab her.

Irish mothers are more protective than any species in the world. Never mind tigers or crocodiles, have you crossed an Irish mother in the wild? There have been times when I was 100 per cent in the wrong and my mother still took my side.

Having said that, she was always straight with me. She never sugar-coated anything. At a hurling match other parents would be cheering, 'Go on, Jimmy, you're brilliant!' If I was crap, my mam would let me know, and if she said I was good, then I knew I was really good. My mother would turn into Ger Loughnane after a match. She'd dissect every pass and score and, to be fair to her, she knew her stuff. Thankfully she left the whole wrestling the opposition's selector thing behind her, but she taught me how to look after myself on the pitch. She must have been proud when the next time an opposition manager called me a fat bastard, I ended up fighting him on the sideline myself. He must have been forty-five. At the time, my mother had just had my little sister, so she refrained from jumping the fence. There's only so much you can do with a six-month-old beside you in a carrycot. That child must have been at every pitch in north Tipperary before she was a year old. (Actually I've just remembered now that my mother wasn't happy following that incident, she gave me a stern talking to when I got home, but I still reckon she was secretly buzzing.)

My mam always insists that my sister, Abi, and I do our best at everything. 'Do your best and God will do the rest' was another one of her quotes. Although I don't think God has ever done Vicar Street. I think she mostly wanted to motivate me. If you tried, that'd be something. For example, if I had my hands on my hips during a game, she'd go mental and roar at me, 'Get your hands off your hips!' Soccer was worse. I'd be up front, and the ball wouldn't always be up that end of the pitch – I'd have to wait for it, so I'd have my hands on my hips. At full-time my mam would say, 'I'm not watching this crap. You had your hands on your hips all day, like a teapot. I'm not paying in for this.'

It didn't matter who the opposition was. It could be a street league, and she'd still be as animated. Recently I went to watch my sister play a soccer match, and Mam said, 'Ah, I've calmed down a lot these days, John.' Absolute lie. There were more people at the game to watch my mam going mental than there were to watch the soccer. To be fair to her, she was a good player too. I remember watching her at a pupil–staff soccer match and she was the best of the women. I was proud as punch. She never shouted at her teammates, though. That was just for her kids.

Usually when Mam shouted at me, it drove me on to play better. Abi is the opposite. She needs an arm around the shoulder, while I need tough love. One day I was having a nightmare and I walked over to the dugout and told Mam to fuck off. She said nothing but gave me a look – that look. After that, I swear I didn't want the game to end. Afterwards she said, 'Don't you shout at me in front of everyone. There was a solicitor there. What will he think of us?' It wasn't what I had said; it was who I said it in front of. Irish mammies all over the country love keeping up appearances. Pure Hyacinth Bucket job.

My mam always reckoned I was a bit soft as a young lad. When I was twelve, I hurt my hand playing AstroTurf soccer. I went home and complained about the wrist for three or four days, until she relented and brought me to the A&E in Nenagh. We didn't have a car at the time, so it was a bit of an ordeal to get there. Mam said to me in the waiting room, 'There better be something wrong with you.' So when the doctor said it was only bruised, nothing broken, Mam said, 'I told ya. You're a hypochondriac.'

To be fair, I kind of was. She says that all through my childhood I was obsessed with bandages. I'd let on that I'd hurt my hand so that I'd get a bandage on it. I think I just liked the look of them. Anyway, after another two or three weeks of cycling around on my bike and trying to play hurling, my wrist was still killing me. Whenever I complained, Mam would say, 'Sure, there's nothing wrong with ya. You heard the doctor.' Then the hospital rang back to say they had mixed up my X-ray and that my wrist was actually broken. I had to go back to Nenagh and then to Limerick to get a cast. I got a few bars of chocolate for that one.

My mam also wanted to make sure we were independent when we were young. When I was about nine, she took me to the barber, and the barber looked at her and asked, 'What does he want?'

She'd said, 'Tell him what you want, John.'

I said, 'Go-faster stripes and a Ronaldo fringe.'

Mam said, 'He'll have a short back and sides.'

But at least I was learning. Learning that my mother was the boss.

In some houses, it was 'Wait until I tell your father,' but in our house, there was no need for waiting. My mam was mother, father, sergeant, judge, jury and executioner, the whole lot. My poor father wouldn't get a word in edgeways.

My mam is funny. She is actually sound. But like every Irish mammy, no one is good enough for her son. If I brought Beyoncé home, she'd say, 'Ah, I'd have rathered Katy Perry.'

The best thing about Mam is that she finds me funny, and that's why we're so close. When she went to my sixth-year parent–teacher meeting and a teacher said, 'Jonathan thinks I fancy him,' Mam thought it was hilarious. I was outside handing out leaflets because I was a prefect, so there I was waving in at my mam and my teacher. The teacher thought it was quite serious, but my mam was just laughing away.

The great thing is that I feel I can talk to her about anything. When I was thirteen, she knew exactly who

I was texting and shifting, and if she didn't like them, she'd let me know. But at the same time, she never forced me to do anything and always insisted I make my own mistakes. She used to clean my room, too, and one day I was surprised to find a box of condoms in my drawer. When I asked her about it, she said, 'I don't wanna know what you're at, but I don't want to be a grandmother.' Understood. No need for any more chat on that.

'Your mammy is always right' and 'liars will always be found out' are two more of Mam's catchphrases. Even just recently she put me on the phone to my younger sister and I had to remind Abi that, yes, Mammy is always right.

She did get one thing wrong, though. When I was fourteen, I bought an electric guitar and an amp from Argos. I couldn't play a note on the guitar and it being right-handed and me being left-handed didn't help. I just kind of wanted it. It looked cool in my room. Maybe I'd have a girl over and she'd say, 'Oh my God, do you play guitar?' Then I'd be like, 'No.' So I quickly gave up on the guitar, but I realized that I could plug a microphone into the amp and sing along to karaoke on YouTube. Obviously the amp made my out-of-tune singing even louder – brilliant. I sang everything, from Van Morrison to Westlife . . . badly. Then I'd hear the Bang! Bang! Bang! – the sweeping brush clattering against the ceiling below, followed by the mother shouting, 'Shut up that noise. Jesus, Jonathan, I'm begging ya.' She said straight out that I was useless. Now whenever she hears me sing she makes a point of telling me how good I am, maybe in the hope that I'll forget that she tried to crush my dreams. I know she loves me, really. When we asked her if it was OK to put these stories in the book she said, 'Can you not just talk about something else? You'll make me out to be a terrible mother.' Sorry, Mam. You're great.

Mothers will do anything for their kids, though. When I was sixteen, I got my mam to ring in sick to work for me. She told them I had diarrhoea. I didn't. Liverpool were playing Chelsea in Super Sunday and I wanted to see the match and not be stuck behind the counter in SuperValu. At first she said no way, but I knew she would do anything for her son. She's also a Liverpool fan, and during the negotiations I threw into the bargain that I'd hoover the stairs.

This supports my theory that wives replace mammies. Fast-forward eight years and I had dropped out of college but still insisted on living in Waterford, where all my college friends were. I got a job in Foot Locker but was still living the college lifestyle. My first day of work was a Friday. When I came home after work, there was no one in the house. Obviously all my college friends had gone home for the weekend. I hadn't thought this through and I instantly wanted to move home, so I convinced my girlfriend to ring my manager and tell him I'd fallen in the snow and broken my leg. She did it. That was it. I never set foot in Foot Locker again and I moved home after one day's work. This proves my point.

We've both got loads of habits we've picked up and things we've learned from our mammies.

JS: CLEANLINESS: my mother is an animal for cleaning. Before she puts the dishes in the dishwasher, they are already cleaner than any you'd find in a restaurant. I swear to God you'd eat your dinner off our kitchen floor. When I was studying to be a butcher, there was a module on hygiene, and I could have taught it.

JS: FUNNINESS: She's quite good at ranting, which is a skill I've practised numerous times on our podcast. It's kind of her way of expressing herself, a bit like a female Roscrea version of Bill Burr. She always drummed into me that I had to go to school, even when I didn't want to, and she tried to make me study. She slowly realized books weren't for me, but she wanted me to get a good job and she said no one wants to end up working in a shop like she did, which is exactly what I did for a while.

JS: MANNERS: 'It costs nothing to be nice' is a phrase I've heard a million times in my life. It's another one of Mam's favourites. She loves good manners. I think the biggest buzz she gets comes from people telling her I'm nice. Someone might have met me on the street and then told her I had manners, and that means more to her than any amount of number 1 songs or anything. She always insisted I said hello to everyone and learned how to hold a conversation. She'd say, 'You'll go places, you've got the gift of the gab.' That's a very nice way of saying I'm class at talking shite.

JB: SAVING MONEY: *When we were young, we weren't allowed go to the ice-cream van. Maybe it was because Mam was very health-conscious, but more likely it was because she considered the price of a Mr Whippy outrageous. She'd buy a block of ice cream and a packet of wafers in the supermarket, and then when we'd be out in the garden pretending to be Native Americans* or whatever, she'd open the window and pretend to be a shop. Ice cream served, 50 p saved. We weren't paying for Mr Whippy to get a new van, the robbing bastard.

JS: I think all mammies love to save a few bob. When we went shopping for my shoes as a child, I remember the day I went from kids' shoes – size 5½ – to adult shoes – size 6. The price went up about 50 per cent, and my mother was crestfallen. Also this happened when I was about four – I had giant feet. When I was twelve years old, I had size 12 feet.

JB: COOKING: *My mam could make dinner out of a butcher's apron. She'd only be in the door and there'd be spuds on the table four minutes later. I think she'd just tell the spuds to be hot and they'd do it, afraid to argue with her. We were a big spud family. Every day was spud day. When I was about fourteen, rice landed on our dinner table as if from another planet. We had family over from Australia, and after staying with us for a few weeks, they wanted to cook for everyone on their last night. A lovely idea, we thought. They served up a fancy, nutritious curry. After about twenty minutes, my father broke and had to go and sneak a few spuds into him. Mam always kept a stash of cooked potatoes on the top shelf of the fridge, just in case, like. We as a nation then wonder why English people slag us for our spud addiction. There were always carrots, too, a constant stream of veg.*

There was never a bottle of fizzy orange seen in our house, and then at a birthday party one would appear and I'd try to hide my excitement from my friends. They probably had Coke and Fanta at their houses all the time, but I was like an addict getting a fix. I'd drink Country Spring and cheap knock-off Coke till I was sick.

For birthday parties, my mam used to bake a cake shaped in the numerals of your age. Ten and eleven were handy, but by age twelve the tradition went out the window: 'You're old enough. Here's a tart and a candle.' There was always tart. I swear to God she must have had tart in her pocket going around the place. Like in the old westerns where a slick gambler has a gun on some spring-loaded contraption, faster than you could say 'no thanks', there'd be a slice of tart pointed at you, point blank.

Any visitors would get the good teapot, and if Mam served milk in a jug, you knew she was really ramping it up. The tart would be served on little plates that had fancy drawings on them, and then the fancy plates would disappear until the next illustrious guest arrived.

Her thinking was anything cooked at home couldn't be bad for you. Sweets bought in the shop were only full of sugar and E's – the flavourings and additives, not the illegal pills. If it was baked at home, it was good for you, regardless of how much sugar and butter went into it. That's mammy science.

Mothers are great for when you're sick. They have the wildest home remedies. You know the teabag on your eye to get rid of a stye? My mother invented that. She once said to me, 'I got these teabags in the shop. If you take these, you'll never be sick.' My mam was a nurse; these were teabags. She has a cure for everything – sometimes scientific, sometimes mammy science.

Most mammies are class at knitting, patching, sewing and all that. Turning up school pants? Not a bother to her. She'd fix anything. Maybe she didn't want to spend money on new school pants, maybe buying fewer pants was good for the environment, or maybe she just wanted to be busy. No one knows and no one needs to know. When your mother says, 'Give me that jumper,' you give it to her. She'll do her magic on it and that's it.

If I said I was going to the moon to fight robot Nazis, Mam would say, 'Well, bring a jacket.'

'You're going to America on tour? Have ya sandwiches?' You couldn't go to America or the moon without sandwiches. This may explain why I bring sandwiches on the plane with me. Smacks says it's illegal and I shouldn't get through airport security with them, but aeroplane food is generally terrible and my body is 40 per cent homemade sandwiches. A lack of sandwiches could prove fatal. Stopping at the shop and buying a roll is not an option. Rolls can probably kill you and/or are a waste of money. I never really got to the bottom of that one.

Mammies should also have their own dictionary. Mammy language. My mam calls the amusements and roller-coasters in Tramore 'Zipadeedoodahs'. They're also on the danger list, along with being outside without a hat (as a teenager I grew my hair long and no one knew because I always had a woolly hat on) and steak that is cooked any way other than extremely well done.

'The French eat it pink in the middle, Mam.'

'They'll all die from that one of these days.'

'They've been doing it for hundreds of years.'

'No, it's disgusting. They're lucky to be alive.'

She also despises shorts. Anyone wearing shorts will definitely catch a chill and die. On a field during a game is OK, or on holidays in Spain, but other than that, they will cause immediate death by exposure.

Sometimes I see kids out in just a jumper and think there's no way that would have gone on when I was small. Coats were like parachutes – just pull a cord and a coat would appear. If it turned out that my mam was a secret agent/ninja before she had me, that would explain a lot. Perhaps her speciality was turning the spy headquarters into a kitchen in thirty seconds before the cops arrived. Nothing to see here, just sandwiches.

If my mam sees you in a crowd, you will see her too. She'll wave like she's trying to land a fighter jet. Apparently you can see the Great Wall of China from space, but I reckon if my mam wanted to catch your attention, astronauts could be passing overhead and say, 'Wait, is that Mrs O'Brien waving at us?' It is, lads, you forgot your sandwiches.

Some mammies get into hobbies like flower-arranging and unnecessary amounts of baking. My mam is mad for hobbies. She can paint pictures, sing, knit anything into anything, grow flowers out of your ear, play the piano and line dance. She's done night courses in things I can't pronounce. She even did reiki for a while. Looking back now, I realize it's because I was a hyperactive child and she may have just wanted to get out of the house for a bit. She gets bored after a month and moves on to the next one.

Sometimes we think our mas were just born mammies, that they came out of the womb asking the doctor why none of the staff had warm hats on. It can shock us to learn that our parents were once young, perhaps even stylish. My mam said she used to have an afro. I saw *the photo, and it turns out she had a perm. This makes me question the 'Your mammy knows everything' bit, Smacks. But they definitely know where everything is. If anything couldn't be found in twenty seconds, we'd shout, 'MMMMAAAAAAAAA!' She'd know exactly where the lost object was, without even looking. Before there was Google, there was Mammy. Before it was, 'Alexa, what time does the shop open?' or 'How long does it take to roast a chicken?' you could just ask Mammy.*

Mammies' Achilles' heel is that they think their sons will grow up to be Superman, or at least to be better than their fathers. But this is based on absolutely zero evidence. Maybe they hope that if they can just mash enough spuds and iron enough shirts for them, their sons won't go to jail. Their tactics change depending on which sibling they're dealing with. The eldest child is often the leader – they're more independent, more competitive in sport, etc, and they'll probably need less intervention. But by the time Mammy has the youngest son, she realizes he's the last and puts extra effort into him, like a GAA coach saying, 'This is the last run, lads. Give it everything.' He's the one most likely to know how to cook and how to never have to cook.

If you're still brushing your son's hair when he's a teenager, it may already be too late.

I better stop telling stories about my mam now, just to be safe. One of her favourite sayings is, 'Be good to your mother or she'll spend your inheritance on a nursing home.'

JS: My mam has become a bit of a cult favourite with 2 Johnnies fans. She appears most weeks on our xtra podcast. She's even got her own segment called 'Well, Trish', with her own theme music and everything. She reckons she's going to be the next Kris Jenner. Every week she has everyone in stitches with her crazy stories, and mostly just embarrasses me. There's only one way to close out this chapter and that's with some of our favourite tales from Trish. Her take on the world is nearly as crazy as ours, and we love her for it.

On protecting Smacks when he was young

Jonathan was down the road pucking a ball against the wall, and these two young lads, hardy boys, cool kids, came down and started taking the ball off him. Acting the eejit, ya know. And Jonathan was like a little sheep, saying nothin'. So I saw it and sort of . . . lost the head, as usual, and ran down, and Jonathan just stood there. The two boys saw me coming and I ran after them off down towards the playground. I caught one of them by the jumper. I just said, 'Don't ever effin' come round here ever again tormenting my boy,' and he said, 'Ah, Trisha, Trisha, I swear it wasn't me. It was the other lad.' And I said again, 'Don't ever come round here again.' And that was it. To this day the young lad says, 'Well, Trisha, how are you?' And he's a grown man now, obviously.

On her fitness regime

I actually put on a bit of Joe Wicks because I think he's a bit of a fine thing. Three days into it I said, 'Ah, feck this!' I hurt some part of my leg and I was crippled. I couldn't walk up the stairs. I said I'd just look at him but I wouldn't do the exercises. So instead now in the mornings I'm drinking tea and eating toast with Joe Wicks.

On Smacks' fashion sense

Well, I'll tell you one thing, I'll always remember when you went off on a bus with your friend when you were about thirteen. These crisis years of thirteen and fourteen! Ye men are always in those crisis years! Off Johnny went with his friend Robert, off to Portlaoise. And this was a big thing, ya know? You were buzzing and I was like, 'Am I off my head now letting these off?' But anyway, in the evening I went down to collect you and, sure, ya know yourself, you got into the car and when I was going up the road I looked at you and I said, 'Holy Jesus!' and I nearly crashed the car! An earring in each ear! Ya know those sparkling ones? Ya know that fella that used to sing there years ago – 60 Cent? Or is it 50 Cent? Yeah, you were like him. I said, 'Get them out! Get them out!' He told me he wanted to look like Nicky Byrne. Well, I'll tell you, you were more like Mary Byrne. You were like a woman! But he had me wrapped around his finger and in the end I let him keep one.

On Smacks arriving home drunk

See I was clever, as you know. I wouldn't give you a key, so I had to answer the door when you'd come home. And, sure, this night, anyway, you were at the door, saying, 'Ah, Mam, I love you.' The usual craic. Drink talk, as they say. I said, 'Get in here, you!' And off he went. He had chips in his hands and he just left them down and said, 'I'm going to bed, Ma.' I was just sitting down myself when I heard a bang. I said, 'Ah, holy mother of Jaysus, what's going on?' I jumped out of the bed, and there he was on the floor. And you know mothers, now? I was saying, 'You're never drinking again. You're never going out again. I'm never giving you money, and that's it.' Anyway, he was trying to get up, and I was trying to lift him up, and the next thing is he banged off the desk. The computer went flying onto the ground. My blood pressure was really up now at this stage, 'cause you know I'm not really into drink, you know what I mean? This was really bugging me.

Then he got sick everywhere. Oh my God, I lost the plot, but thank God you learned after that. But I made him suffer the next day. I made him eat a big dinner. I was enjoying watching the sweat bucketing off him at the kitchen table. He never done it again. He knew better. He wouldn't have been let into the house.

On the birds and the bees

Oh, I'd say he knew a fair bit, but anyway, in them days it was kinda hard, so me and my friend were talking and I said I think I'll get him a book. Be done with it, ya know? Eason's was only getting big at that time. The big one was in Dublin, so me and my friend went off on the bus to get this book. We eventually got through about twenty of them and we brought home one, and I said to him, 'John, I'm leaving something in your room there. If you get a chance, just have a look at it.'

He said, 'Ah, Mam, what is it?'

I think he thought it was a pair of jeans or something. Off he went up to the room anyway and, sure, after a few minutes didn't the lads arrive at the door.

'C'mon upstairs, lads, c'mon,' he said.

And here I was: 'Ah, Jesus Christ almighty tonight.'

Then all I could hear was the laughs and the skits coming from the room. I was banging on the door, saying, 'C'mon out of there now, ye.'

The boys were well informed of the birds and the bees, I'll tell you. I reckon Jonathan knew too. He was just playing dumb. Like all ye fellas, I think he learned it all from films. Well, he had this boxset at home, right? *American Pie* was the name of it – I'll always remember it – and every night he used to put it on the aul telly that he had in the room. And I used to say to David, 'How does he watch the same thing over and over again?' He was laughing, and said, 'Sure, isn't he happy?' Well, it was only a few years later I knew what the craic was with *American Pie*.

We want to take this opportunity to thank our mammies for making us what we are today. We wouldn't be where we are without ye. Also, please don't be offended by anything we said. Although it's all true.

HOW TO BE A ROCKSTAR

JB: *Dundrum, west Tipperary, a sleepy village, home to P. P. O'Dwyer's hardware store, Crowe's pig farm, and a GAA team known as the Hockers. The latest census puts the population at 165. So it was certainly a surprise to us when, in the late nineties, one of the biggest nightclubs in Munster opened in Dundrum. It was called Bucks. Once a month it held a teenage disco, a chance for lads from all over the county to fight and try to shift a bird from Cashel. Being a bit of a hairy, black-hoodie-wearing lad who was in a noisy rock band, I only went once, because my best mate, Gonzo, talked me into it.*

Around this time, four young lads from Dublin, going by the name No Angels, became a busking sensation and reached number 5 in the Irish charts with their cover of The Beatles' 'Help!' And as fate would have it, the night we went to the teenage disco, they were putting on a very special event: No Angels, an actual band, would play on stage before the DJ launched into four hours of Vengaboys. Gonzo saw this, walked up to the bouncer and asked, 'Who owns this place?' The bouncer was taken aback, but after a while he brought us up to meet the manager. Gonzo said, 'How's it going? Here, we're in a band and we're better than those useless bastards.' He

*pointed at the pop sensations on stage. 'Give us a gig
and we'll have the place hoppin''.' Four minutes later, we
were booked to play the next teenage disco: Junior Cert
results night. 1,500 teenagers raring to go. It was going
to be wild.*

*We arrived in the back of Uncle Buddie's van and
tried to act like we had a clue what we were doing
during soundcheck. Then it was showtime. We blasted
into a mix of Green Day, Blink 182 and a song we wrote
ourselves about how it was bad luck to go to school on
Friday the thirteenth. Thirty minutes in and the crowd of
peaked-cap-wearing, eyebrow-slit-sporting hard chaws
were getting restless.*

'This is a disco, not Wayne's World,' said one lad.

*The bouncers told us to pack up and the Vengaboys
kicked in.*

*We grabbed our gear and started running it out to
the big blue van, pulling our hoods up against the heavy
rain. When I got back to the door we'd been loading out
of, a big bouncer grabbed me and said, 'Hey, where do
ya think you're going?'*

*A garda intervened, put her hand on the bouncer's
shoulder and said the immortal words: 'It's OK. He's in
the band.'*

I was fourteen years old. My life was changed forever.

Choose your weapon

Picking your instrument is step one. Most young
lads want to play guitar or drums. If your family has
a garage, maybe you can be a drummer. If not, it's
guitar time.

We always wondered how lads end up playing

the bass. Remember when you were playing soccer as a kid and no one wanted to go in goal? Bass is the musical equivalent of going in goal.

Keyboards are very sensible, like if Denis Irwin was an instrument. They make perfect sense as an adult, but at thirteen we'd never seen any cool dudes smash a piano at a gig.

If you're lucky enough to be in a family that likes traditional Irish music, then happy days! You'll have flutes and fiddles in your pram. An all-rounder.

The guitar is like an attacking midfielder. Roy Keane would have been a guitar player, like Slash without the fags. Paul Scholes: the Noel Gallagher of football.

But Georgie Best and Eric Cantona, they would be frontmen, whether they could sing or not. There would be no point trying to coach them, just let them off to score goals and impress women.

A friend of ours started learning the bagpipes. The Scouts were starting a pipe band and for some Jaysus reason he came home with the big bag of Scottish mayhem. His mother wouldn't let him practise in the house, so every evening he'd march up and down the estate playing the bagpipes. We don't need to tell you, lads, a beginner on the bagpipes is a formidable neighbour. Not once did anyone try and shoot him, which just goes to show what a nice town Cahir is. Bagpipes are the Paul McShane of instruments.

JS: In secondary school I tried to learn loads of instruments but none of them worked out well for me. I even gave the tin whistle a good rattle but I had to stop because my mother hated the sound of it. I got a bad note sent home from my music teacher one time and I had to get my mam to sign it. Poor Miss Kinane wanted me to practise the tin whistle every night but my mother said I'd have to move out if I wanted to pursue my tin whistle career. I must have been fairly bad at it.

The realization hit me in sixth year that I wasn't going to be a pop star. So I decided to go down another route. A group of lads in my year had started a band, and I thought I'd fit perfectly as head of security. They organized a gig in our local town hall and I convinced them to let me organize the security. I roped in my cousin, who was a security guard at the time, and the two of us worked the door for the night. I felt invincible and let the role go to my head a bit. I threw out three of my friends for smoking. I even spoke like a bouncer. 'All right there, folks' and 'Not tonight' suddenly became part of my vocabulary, even though I'd only been a security guard for fifteen minutes. Monday morning in school was fairly awkward after that.

Picking your bandmates

JB: *Ideally you want someone who has a shed. My mate James liked music and his parents were building a shed on a field next to their house – an ideal spot to bang the drums. I wasn't great but I was determined. We took a break for Christmas. Then in January I realized James hadn't practised at all over the holidays. He had to get the boot from the band. It was just a coincidence that his parents had sold the shed.*

Gonzo had a shed, and the fact that he played guitar was a bonus. However, he had a habit of sticking his tongue out when he had to concentrate on a chord change. It didn't look fantastic but he got the job done.

Gonzo introduced me to an older boy from school who played guitar and even owned a half-decent amp. He was definitely in the band. He insisted on bringing his dodgy-looking mate to be the bass player. He couldn't play bass and he scared the shit out of me, but he was in too. He also had a shed, but you wouldn't go into it.

As you get older, your criteria for bandmates change. You want a lad who has a car, because your parents will surely get sick of driving you around, and rocking up with your parents is a bad look for future rock 'n' roll legends. You wouldn't see Metallica arrive at a gig in their ma's Corolla.

I knew a lad called Petey Starlet, who owned about five Toyota Starlets in a row. He could play guitar, but we didn't need a guitarist, so he transferred to bass and was in the band. Then we met Mikey, who was an apprentice electrician and owned a van. He was absolutely in the band.

First gig

Hopefully your town is lucky enough to have somewhere a new band can play. Our towns had parish halls that sometimes hosted battles of the bands. The venues sat somewhere between a teenage disco and Slane, if Slane was sixty lads in a hall. Town halls tend to have the acoustics of a tin of dog food, and Bruno Mars wouldn't sound good in there, but we can't recommend them enough. The biggest learning curve for any band is their first gig, even if it's in a hall that only six hours earlier hosted the ICA's country market.

JB: *Every band needs an angle, perhaps a gimmick. Ours was that for the last song I wouldn't play guitar. Instead we'd do a rap song and I'd just go mental on the mic. I once got a bit carried away and stage-dived off the 5 ft panto stage onto a few first years. This was at a fundraising gig for the ladies' football club. Their chairman was a big man and he ran in to break up the mosh pit I was starting. He scolded us after that and told us we had a lovely little band but that I was going to fucking ruin it with that carry-on. He asked me to present the medals to the U16s a few years ago and made a speech about what a great young man I was. I couldn't help but laugh then, and I hope he gets a laugh out of reading this now.*

We didn't win the battle of the bands; it was won by a band who were actually good. But our guitar player got the shift off a decent-looking young wan from out Clogheen direction. We thought we were Guns N' Roses.

At our first pub gig a massive brawl erupted. At this stage the band was called Sean Aeglish (we saw it on a sign and thought it sounded cool. It turns out it's Irish for 'old church' – class!). My proud mam was sitting down the back with a camcorder, and halfway through 'Sweet Home Alabama' a man backed into camera shot with a bar stool over his head shouting, 'I'll kill you, you cunt!' We played on as we'd been practising for six months since our battle of the bands defeat, and four men needed hospitalization after a mass brawl wasn't going to distract us from going from D to C to G over and over again. It just added to our legend, and there was a right crowd at our second gig, probably hoping to see a scrap. No such luck.

JS: My fledgling career started when I was seven and my mother used to get me to dress up as Garth Brooks and perform live in The Hogan Stand Bar (now The Stand Bar) in Roscrea. Most Sunday afternoons I'd stroll out from the ladies' toilet dressed head to toe in cowboy gear, complete with the Stetson hat and my mother's boots – the whole shebang. I then proceeded to murder three or four of Garth Brooks's well-known hits, which were received with great enthusiasm by my adoring fans, who comprised my mother and a few neighbours and friends. But who cares? I was up and running and stardom awaited.

My music career hit the rocks for a few years, but at twelve I bounced back, wowing my relatives at Christmas with my version of 'Build Me up Buttercup'. That Christmas I decided to get a karaoke machine. My friends laughed me out of it at the time; they were getting go-karts and remote-control cars, and I was inside thinking I was Gary Barlow.

JB: *I'll always remember one of my early pub gigs. I was probably only fifteen and our band was fairly rough. We thought we were set for stardom. It was a Sunday afternoon and we were bashing away at 'Born to Be Wild', blowing the heads off the ten or twelve lads in the pub, when BANG! There was a loud thud. Our bass player had broken a string. The band stopped and he shouted, 'Faaaaaakkk!' He didn't have a spare. We had a quick band meeting live on stage about what to do.*

At this point the whole place had gone silent and was watching to see what we'd do next. I approached the mic and said, 'Sorry! Technical difficulties.' Auld Paddy Corbett shouted up from the bar, 'Ah, lads, MTV just walked out the fuckin' door!'

JS: The first time I ever sang properly in front of friends was during transition year in school. We were on a religious retreat and they were looking for someone to sing a song at the ceremony. 'OK, course,' deluded me obliged. There was method to my madness, though. I knew that singers and musicians got all the girls, and having just broken up with my girlfriend, I thought this was the perfect way to win her back. It worked a treat. She fell for it, hook, line and sinker, as I serenaded her and the rest of transition year in with Leonard Cohen's hit 'Hallelujah'.

Image

A band's image is very important. When Picture This arrive onstage in oversized pink suits and black nail polish, you know they're in a super-cool pop band . . . or on a stag gone wrong. But they definitely stand out.

JB: *For our first pub gig, we didn't quite think it through. We all wore black, kind of by accident, except Gonzo, who wore a brown fleece (I think he came straight from work). He was playing bass and I was the rhythm guitarist, but he insisted I learn the set list on bass too 'in case he got caught up in a session' and I had to cover him.*

Having a band photo is essential. Getting in the local paper used to be like winning a Grammy for a young band. Nowadays people have fantastic artsy photos they post on Instagram. All we had was my ma's analogue camera. You'd go to SuperValu a week later to collect your photos and realize you didn't look as cool as Oasis.

How to take the perfect band photo

THE TRADITIONAL LINE-UP: Like *The Usual Suspects,* usually against a wall. Someone will probably put one leg against the wall. You might even wear sunglasses. Don't all look at the camera; you're too cool for that. The straight line suggests ye mean business, but it's not the most creative, making it ideal for lazy cover bands (like the ones JB was in).

THE EPIC SHOT: Could be in an old castle or church, possibly a field or a quarry. (Don't ask your mam to walk around a quarry all day.) Guys wearing jeans, legs spread in the power stance like they're about to shoot you with their manliness. This worked for a bit in the nineties; now it's for bikers and heavy metal bands.

COOL DUDES: The urban rapper style. Hand signs are to be avoided unless you are actually sign-languaging your band's name. Five teenagers from Longford pulling the 'Westside' hand sign will become a meme that will follow you long after you've given up and become a dentist.

SEX SELLS: Getting young wans in bikinis to be in your photos and music videos kind of works if you're Biggie Smalls, but if the poor girl is on the bonnet of a Toyota Celica for two hours while ye shoot the video and photos, she'll be perished. You'd juice oranges off her nipples. What works in Hollywood, California, doesn't necessarily work in Hollywood, County Wicklow.

Our advice? Be yourself. If you don't have a big budget, keep it simple.

JB: *You know the way rappers like Nelly always wore basketball and American football gear and people thought they were cool? Do you reckon people think I'm cool because I wear GAA jerseys every day?*

JS: Well, the Tipp jersey is the same colour as the Golden State Warriors of San Francisco, so you never know. But I highly doubt it.

The X Factor

JS: I always wanted to be a rock star; I just wasn't willing to put in the work. I remember watching *The X Factor* in 2004 and deciding then and there, never mind the work, *Sure, I'll just win that.* I genuinely thought it would be that easy. I'd just rock up to the audition and blow away Simon Cowell and the other judges. I remember looking at James Arthur and thinking, *That's easy. I can do the exact same.* I had overlooked two little things: he had massive talent and an incredible voice, and I . . . well, I had neither. But I didn't get bogged down in the small stuff. And if for some strange reason I didn't win *The X Factor*, I'd surely win *The All Ireland Talent Show*, which was on around that time. (Again, deluded.)

JB: *I once auditioned for* You're a Star, *which was basically the Irish equivalent of* The X Factor. *I didn't enter as a solo singer but as part of a three-piece rock* band called Red River. We arrived on to the RDS in Dublin, where the show was being filmed. Our bass player was late as he'd been at Electric Picnic on a major lash, and when he eventually arrived, it was clear he did not look like a star. The grass stains on his pants made it look like he'd been in goal for a marathon game of World Cup down the estate, and his hair smelled of dandelions and cider. We gave him sunglasses to hide his bloodshot eyes and asked him to adopt a silent/mysterious persona during our performance. He was actually a very talented bass player when he was sober, but he'd no real interest in reality TV competitions.

When judge Brendan O'Connor asked, 'Will ye be able to control that fella?' all I could say was, 'Ah shur, doesn't he control himself?' But he got into a debate with the judges about conspiracy theories, called Eurovision winner Linda Martin a 'shape-shifting lizard', insisted that RTÉ were part of the Illuminati and said Linda was one of the aliens responsible for building the pyramids. Just for good measure, he added that her Eurovision song was shite. I had to pull him up on that last one.

We met Kodaline in the waiting room. They were less into conspiracy theories and actually got to the final that year, performing under the name 21 Demands. They've gone on to be one of the biggest Irish bands of all time. Funny how things work out.

We eventually parted ways with our mad bass player. I rang him recently and during our chat I asked if he played the bass any more.

He said, 'I hadn't played in about two years, then I picked it up the other day and I was still class, so I put it down again.'

The equipment

An Argos guitar amplifier might be loud enough to blow the ears off you, but for singing you need to spend a few euro on good gear. If a singer can't hear themselves, they sing louder and often damage their voice.

JB: *You could never hear the singer of the first band I was in. I did backing vocals for six months and it turned out I was singing the wrong lyrics.*

There was a man who used to park up outside Spar of a Friday evening and he sold musical equipment out of the back of his truck. Looking back, it seems a bit dodge. No one knew his name; he was known only as Bumble Bee. He had the most unusual-looking instruments and the strangest brand names you'd ever heard of. It was like the Aldi version of rock 'n' roll and we loved it. Gonzo bought a red bass guitar off him one time. It looked a bit space-aged but it worked fine for years. One night we were all playing a few tunes in a friend's band room (one of the other bands in town were lucky enough to have a cool band room where they could smoke and even sneak in a few cans) and one of our non-musical mates was watching. He said, 'Gonzo, I always thought that red bass guitar looked mental. Would ya not buy a new one?'

Gonzo said, 'Shur, it does the job. Basses don't grow on trees, man. This cost me money.'

'How much?'

'About €150.'

'That was years ago.'

'I'm getting value out of it.'

'Get a new one. Let me smash it, like in the films.'

'No, man. I need it.'

'I'll give you €50.'

'€80.'

'Deal.'

And with that, cash was exchanged and our mate picked up the magic red bass and smashed it off the concrete floor until it was in bits.

'Some craic! Now let's go to the pub.'

Know your audience

JB: While still in school, our band got a gig in the village of Killenaule, in south-east Tipperary. The dad of one of our members was in a cover band and he told us one of his regular pubs had phoned to say they had a cancellation and needed a band to cover. 'No bother,' we said. We got a lift off parents and neighbours and set up in the tiny pub, under the television, where no one could escape us. We played the songs we knew and the crowd were fairly forgiving because we were so young and they were so scuttered. As we hit the last chord of the last song, we breathed a big sigh of relief – we had survived.

The owner came up and said, 'You'll have to play one more.'

'We don't know any more.'

'You'll have to. It's Tom Joe's birthday,' he said, pointing to an elderly man at the bar who looked like Dinny Byrne from Glenroe, complete with flat cap and beer belly.

There was a quick discussion and the crowd started to shout up at us. They could sense we hadn't a clue, and they were getting a great laugh out of it.

'OK,' I said, 'this one is for you. Happy birthday, Tom Joe! Seventy-four today!'

We kicked into the only other song we knew: Metallica's 1983 heavy metal seven-minute masterpiece, 'Seek and Destroy'.

We finished to absolute silence.

'Thank you, and here's to seventy-four more, Tom Joe.'

The first time the two of us performed on stage together was at a Cahir GAA medal presentation night. We had managed to squeeze a few quid out of the club to get a one-man band for after the dinner. The one-man band didn't realize he would be playing to a few hundred people at a GAA function and gave us a look as if to say, 'Ah, lads!' Gigs like these normally require an eight-piece band all working hard to get the crowd out of their chairs and onto the dance floor. A one-man band was going to have his work cut out for him. He had done us a deal on the price, I'd say he regretted it.

JB: *He called me up on stage to sing . . . and get revenge, I suppose. So up I went. But it was a tough crowd and I needed help. I announced over the mic, 'Ladies and gentlemen, will you please go wild for the singing sensation, Roscrea's Ricky Martin – Mr Johnny Smacks!'*

JS: Full to the neck of Coors Light and egged on by my new teammates in Cahir GAA, once again I obliged.

JB: *So Smacks got up and for some reason we decided to sing Paolo Nutini's 'Candy', one of the most depressing songs of all time. We must have been singing it at home* *during the week (we lived together at the time and kitchen karaoke was a regular occurrence). Up onstage, when all eyes are on you, you have to make fast decisions.*

JS: At the time I was obsessed with impersonating other singers, so thinking I was a great fella, I thought all I have to do to get the crowd on side is sing in Paulo Nutini's accent. Of course I forgot to let the crowd in on this joke. They thought I must develop some sort of Scottish twang whenever I'm drunk and they didn't know what was going on.

JB: *People clapped, a little unsure of what had just happened. In the following week's newspaper, my father, Ger, had written up the Cahir notes and said, 'Johnny Smacks wowed the crowd with his fabulous stagecraft.' That was one way of putting it.*

JS: It's now nine years later and I still haven't won them over, but thanks anyway, Ger.

GAA SUNDAYS

Croke Park, 3.30 p.m., 19 August 2018. It is warm and humid, what we call 'close' weather for some reason, as if the clouds are in the room with you. We are rethinking our decision to wear suits, as the shirts are sticking to our backs and a large man from Pallasgreen is involuntarily jostling us every time the ball moves. He has a green and white headband around his wrist and he kind of smells of onions (probably had a burger from a chip van on the way in). The game starts fairly hectic. Limerick's young guns are firing, and the enormity of the occasion shows no signs of affecting them as they go into half-time up by 4 points – 1–10 to Galway's 9 points. We manage to get a pint in at half-time, feeling very privileged to be here, considering our own county isn't involved, bar the assistant referee, who lives down the road from us, but you wouldn't be getting dressed up for him. On the way in we saw grown men trying to sell their oldest sons for a terrace ticket: 'He's good to work and doesn't eat much.' We'd pulled more strings than a harp player to secure ours. We even talked our way into a hospitality lounge, where we stealthily picked up two bottles of beer each and put a few sneaky vol-au-vents in our pockets for later (you never know).

Limerick don't have a pint at half-time; they have a

serious look at themselves and come out determined to break the hoodoo Croke Park has had on them in the past. They roar into a 9-point lead. Surely Galway, the defending All-Ireland champions, are dead and buried. They dog it back to five, then with only two minutes to go, off the Limerick bench comes the solid figure of Shane Dowling. He was the first name on the team sheet for so long, but a lingering injury put him on crutches for months and he's been relegated to being an impact man, and man, what an impact he has! Bang, he slaps a ball low into the right-hand corner of the net and the Treaty side are back 8 points to the good.

Then over the tannoy a voice booms, 'There will be eight minutes of extra time.' Everyone looks at each other. In 1994 Limerick had been 5 points up with five minutes to go. Offaly came back and won by 6 points. Devastating stuff. Limerick hasn't been the same since. Into extra time we slip, Galway's Conor Whelan pulls a ball out of the air and smashes it into the net. *Here we go again!* Joe Canning gets a 21-yard free and fizzes it to the top-left corner. Only two points in it now. *Holy Jaysus!* Galway's Niall Burke picks up a spilled ball 65 yards out on the Hogan Stand side. *Christ, why is there no one marking him?* He whips it over the bar and we're down to 1 point. It couldn't happen again, could it?

Seven minutes into extra time, Limerick's Graham Mulcahy frantically nips into the corner and squeezes a shot off before two big West of Ireland men devour him. Limerick are back in the lead by two. Half the stadium takes a breath. Joe Canning points a 65, back to one. Then, in the last minute of added time, Galway are awarded a free. It's in their own half of the field, almost on the sideline. To score, it would have to be a mother and father of a shot, but the man taking it is a colossus of hurling, possibly the greatest his county has ever produced, and that's no small feat. Everyone in the stadium seems to get a small electric shock every time he gets the ball. Up steps Joe Canning. If you want anyone to take a free, you want it to be Joe. He's already bagged an impressive goal and 10 points today; what's one more? He lifts the ball, strikes it well. Every eye is glued to the ball. *Jaysus, he's fair far out. He'll never reach the goal. He might.* The ball sails nicely, but between the close weather, God and the fatigue of seventy-eight minutes of battle, Joe drops the ball short. A hand in a green jersey pulls it out of a forest of ash and launches it down the field.

The whistle goes, Limerick are champions. 1897, 1918, 1921, 1934, 1936, 1940, the long wait to 1973 and now in 2018. Captain Declan Hannon climbs the hallowed steps of the Hogan Stand, named after a Tipperary footballer who was shot dead by British troops during a match in 1920. Here we are now, two Tipp men surrounded by a sea of jubilant Limerick fans. Hannon lifts the cup, thanks the people as Gaeilge agus as Bearla. Then from the speakers, starting quietly and rising to thump, comes the sound of Limerick's most-loved band, The Cranberries. They had tragically lost their singer Dolores O'Riordan during the year. The song is 'Dreams'. The crowd sings and there are tears in our eyes as we join in. No one is leaving any time soon. Our county isn't even playing, but they will be someday; someday this will be us. For now, it's going to be one hell of a night. We're glad we wore suits.

The 2 Johnnies' Tips for Inter-County GAA

Get a good run at the day

JS: When you're gearing up for a trip to a game, it's important to get a good start to the day. Do not go out the night before the big game. We know you're not going to be fighting for the breaking ball or contesting puck-outs, but you have to be prepared nonetheless. If you've got eyes like two pool balls hanging out of your head from a night on the razzle-dazzle, you're not going to be much use to anyone and you'll drag everyone else down. Hangovers aren't fun at the best of times and especially not when you've a long journey ahead of you.

We recommend starting the day with an old-school full Irish, with all the trimmings. Make sure you take a couple of slices of bread on board as well; you'll be glad of them later in the day. It's essential you get the soakage in early. A big tradition back in the day was to go to Mass the morning of the big game. People believed that if you said a few prayers then surely you'd secure that much-needed win. This theory has yet to be scientifically proven. If you gave us a choice of God on our side or a full-forward who can score 2–6 from play, I'd take the full-forward all day long. Anyway, in Tipp we were blessed because we had both for years. Our full-forward was the one and only Eoin Kelly, whose nickname was the Son of God. In his heyday 2–6 from play was no bother to him. Right, you've the prayers said and breakfast eaten; you're good to go. One last thing: bring a heap of sandwiches with you. They'll come in very handy, as we'll explain later. But for God's sake, don't bring egg and onion sandwiches – you'll be pure stink.

Wear your colours

JB: *Never let anyone mistake you for the opposition or, God forbid, a neutral. Wear your county colours. There's a great selection of jerseys, jackets, quarter zip, full zip, hoodies, sleeveless jackets, jumpers, woolly hats, peaked hats. You can even get Westmeath underpants now, though it sounds like they might spoil the romance, if you ask me. Then again, she could be wearing an Offaly thong. Now if that wouldn't get a fella going, nothing would. The point being it's easy to wear your county colours with style these days. When we were young, there were only cotton jerseys that turned to lead when they got wet. Some said they could double up as radiation suits for work on nuclear reactors. You wore your jersey, and if it got cold, you got cold.*

I'll never forget the first time I saw a 'player-fit' jersey. It wasn't massive all over. It actually made a lad's arms look strong. I suppose the idea of the player-fit is to make the player look bigger, stronger and more imposing to the opposition. It doesn't have the same effect on men who don't have an inter-county physique, however. The jersey is forgiving, but perhaps not quite forgiving enough for the beer bellies often stuffed into them. We had a friend who used to say he'd wear a medium because 'women love the tight arms'. His belly was at war with the sponsor on the front of the jersey. We talked him up to a large.

Anything in the right colour will do for the match, though. The Boca Juniors soccer team from Argentina wear a blue and yellow kit. Paddy McCarthy, a Cashel man who left west Tipperary for South America in 1900, actually helped found this famous club. McCarthy was a boxer and a teacher by day, and five of his students wanted to set up their own club, which they asked Paddy to coach. The great Diego Maradona later played for the club, though he'd never have to mark J. J. Delaney. There'd be no 'hand of God' against him.

If you're really cool, you might have your county colours in a foreign team, like the Tipperary hurling club in New York, or the Tipperary hurling club in Boston or San Francisco. We're not sure what it is about Tipp lads – no other county does that half as much. But if you arrive at a match in a Tipp New York jersey, you're cool. You've spent a summer away, hurling for a team abroad like you're Ronaldo. No need to tell people it was the junior B team and you only carried the cooler of beers to the games. It's still exotic to the rest of us, and all that matters is the way you tell it.

The Cork lads always have random flags. The Confederate one is banned now, but I've often seen Canada and Austria, and if anyone can explain why there are so many Japanese flags at Cork matches, I'd be very grateful. I once heard a fairly sozzled man from Carrick say, 'Jaysus, I never knew there was so many Japanese people in Cork. They must only come out for the matches.'

For young women the uniform seems to be a child's jersey and white jeans so tight that they must have put them on aged twelve and grew into them, like a rope around a tree. In summer, the jeans can be swapped for denim hot pants. As a seventeen-year-old on the Killinan-end terrace, I can confirm we spent as much time looking at the brown legs around us as we did at the game. Back in the 2000s, Irish teenagers hadn't quite mastered the art of fake tan, and after one particularly heavy shower of rain during a Munster final, the steps of the terrace were a stream of brown water. I'd swear they were tanning themselves with Bisto.

After the film The Dark Knight *came out, a bunch of us painted our faces blue and gold for a match, which was right craic at the time but fairly dour on the way home that night. Men don't carry baby wipes, so think twice before getting the face paint out, or plan ahead. There's a man from Tipp Town called Sid. If you watch any Tipp match, you'll see Sid in the crowd behind the goal in a blue cowboy hat with those cork things hanging off it, his face painted blue and gold like a warrior and a flag on his back like a cape. He's kind of like a superhero. I wonder does he walk around looking normal and then someone in Thurles blows a horn or shines a light into the sky and Sid goes into a cubicle and emerges like a superhero whose special power is the craic. He travels with a man named Sliotar. I suppose Batman had Robin. How are ye, lads?*

There was another terrace stalwart from Toomevara known as The Brush. Back in the noughties, when Ireland was booming and the terraces were rocking, there was always great anticipation in the air at matches. If the cheering and singing went quiet before throw-in, the chant would start with, 'We want The Brush,' at first quiet, then louder, building to 3,000 fans roaring, 'WE WANT THE BRUSH!' Then out of the middle of the terrace and into the sky would shoot up … The Brush! Yes, an actual sweeping brush painted blue and gold. The crowd went wild. We were easily pleased. There was another lad called Braveheart who used to stand on his mate's shoulders and announce the team, roaring at the top of his voice until he was almost hoarse. He'd shout, 'In goal, Brendan Cummins!' and we'd all cheer, and he'd keep going until he had all twenty-eight players and the management announced. He'd collapse out of sight after his mighty role. Then a few minutes later the actual announcements would come over the tannoy and totally kill the buzz.

The more refined gents, perhaps former players themselves, often opt for a shirt and jumper approach, with just a headband of their county colours around their neck like a tie. They wouldn't know about The Brush.

How to get there

GET A BUS: Once you turn eighteen, there's only one thing on everyone's mind: *Now we can finally organize our own bus to the match.* Previous years you've probably got a bus or got a lift off your parents, but there'll be no parents now. You're cutting loose. In essence it's normally a busload of friends, who don't have any kids or responsibilities, off on the lash and to cheer on their county. We haven't gone to a game in this manner in years but we're hell-bent on reviving the group bus experience.

In 2014 we got a bus to Croker. Everyone was in great spirits when our friend Liam screamed out, 'There's a bomb on the bus!' Everyone went completely silent. He then followed up with another roar: 'A SEXBOMB!' And with that he went on to give one of the best renditions of Tom Jones's hit single 'Sexbomb' that anyone has ever heard. You can't beat the bus for the craic.

GET A LIFT: Getting a lift is definitely the way to go when you get that little bit older, because you can park closer to the ground. Unfortunately if you get a lift with someone, you're not the captain of your own ship, so you'd want to be careful who you get in the car with.

JS: When I was a young lad and I started going to games, I used to get a lift with a fella from my local GAA club. He was sound but the fella he brought with him would give a Panadol a headache. Jesus, Brendan could talk. One time, after Tipperary had lost a game in Croke Park to Waterford, we spent seven hours getting from Dublin to Roscrea due to heavy traffic. It normally takes two hours. For the majority of the seven-hour journey, I had to listen to Brendan's conspiracy theory that Tipperary lost the game because Tipp legend Lar Corbett's hurl was too big for him. I considered getting out in Naas and just staying the night there. It was that painful. As if losing to Waterford wasn't bad enough.

JB: *My parents were big fans of getting to the game*

early. If throw-in was half three, we'd leave around Wednesday. We came armed with enough sandwiches to feed the UN. Ham was always the star of the show, but in later years we added cheese. There was talk of coleslaw for a while but it would never survive the heat of the boot during the drive. We had tea and milk in a plastic bottle that I swear was originally filled with holy water. My ma only brought enough milk to do the job; there would be no unused milk going rancid in the car on the way home. She had it down to the millilitre, so if anyone used more than their allotted share of cow juice, they'd be shot and dumped in the River Lee. If you have a relative who lives near the stadium, you park there and get a go of their milk. It's a dangerous game though. I've parked at a house, lured by the promise of fresh rolls, only to discover they eat egg salad or something mental like that and the house is a three-hour walk from the pitch. I swear Joseph and Mary had it handier on the walk to Bethlehem. We could have done with a donkey to carry the sandwiches.

We parked at a cousin's house in Blackrock for a Cork game once. After the match, the crowd all funnelled out, and every time we went around a corner, we lost a few who went the other direction. Eventually it was just my mam and us kids. We turned down a few alleyways, then into an estate, and we realized there was a man – about twenty years of age and half-jarred – following right behind us.

My mam stopped, turned and said sharply, 'Are you OK there?'

'Yeah,' he said, stunned, as though he'd just been hit by a Toyota. 'I was just following ye. Where are ye going?'

Mam named the estate.

'Ah, shite,' he said. 'I'm looking for the Rochestown Park Hotel.'

The hotel was a good four miles in the opposite direction.

Go the night before

Whether you're heading to Galway, Limerick, Dublin, or anywhere else in the country for that matter, heading up the night before can be a great idea. It cuts out the travel on the day and lets you have a much-needed lie in. Getting to experience the night life in that particular place is a bonus but can throw a spanner in the works if you party too hard.

JS: I remember one weekend we went to a Tipp game in Limerick. We went up on the Saturday night to soak in the atmosphere and save us having to wait in traffic on the way into Limerick the following day. How they haven't built a bypass around Tipp Town yet is a mystery. If by any chance the Minister for Transport is reading this book (which we very much doubt), can you please sort this out? It's an urgent matter. When we arrived and got spiced up to head for a jar in Limerick City, we agreed that we would take it handy and not do the dog on it, as they say. My friend Mike, on the other hand, didn't take this approach. He was so hungover the next day that he couldn't face going to the game. As we set out for the stadium, Mike drove past us. He had actually got in his car and was driving back home. He said he couldn't face the heat of being in the Gaelic grounds in the covered stand. On his journey home he picked up a bottle of Lucozade and a chicken roll and watched the game from the comfort of his own couch. A waste of money.

Get the playlist right

Getting the playlist right is the most important part of travelling to a game. All these lads nowadays doing the auld pop dancing, as Noel Furlong would say – the likes of Drake and Post Malone – sure all these fellas aren't going to get you pumped up for a GAA match. Luckily though, we're men in the know. Below we've compiled our top five GAA songs. And before people start messaging us in saying, 'Aw, why isn't "The Green and Red of Mayo" on the list?' and 'Why isn't "The Rose of Mooncoin" in there?' It's simple – they're not proper GAA songs. They're songs about a county or a particular place, granted, but in our eyes they're not proper, official GAA songs. In order to be considered a GAA song, the song must be about a particular team or released in the lead-up to, or aftermath of, an All-Ireland.

JS: I've got this one, John boy, leave it to me. Right, here we go.

Johnny Smacks' Top Five
GAA Tunes

5. Johnny B and the Boogie Men – 'This Could Be Our Year'

Want to see Johnny B with a beard and ponytail and me

looking like a fourteen-year-old? Then look no further. Before The 2 Johnnies existed there was just Johnny B, who fronted a band that released this cracker of a song. I was living with Johnny B at the time and knew all the words from hearing him play the song at home. I fancied myself as a bit of an actor, so Johnny B asked me to be in the video. The song was written as an ode to the Tipperary hurlers, in the hope that 2014 would be the year that Tipp brought home the Liam MacCarthy Cup. Even now, I still listen to this song on the way to matches.

4. The Saw Doctors – 'Maroon and White Forever'

OK, we may have broken our own rules by putting this song in the top five but we weren't going to not put The Saw Doctors on this list. They're our favourite band ever. This song tells the story of guitarist Leo Moran's dream of All-Ireland football glory with his beloved Galway. If you've never heard this before you're in for one hell of a treat.

3. The 2 Johnnies – 'The Premier Rap'

This is the first song we ever produced, during the unforgettable weeks leading up to the 2016 All-Ireland final between Tipperary and Kilkenny. We may have illegally snuck into several locations to film the video – say nothing. It was our take on the nineties classic 'Jump Around' by House of Pain. Thankfully Tipp won and we performed the song in front of 40,000 people in Semple Stadium at the homecoming.

2. Rory and the Island – 'Jimmy's Winning Matches'

In 2012 Donegal came from nowhere to get their hands on the Sam Maguire. Never mind the torturous training Jim McGuinness put the players through, we put all their success down to this belter of a song. It's one of the catchiest songs of all time and the epic music video was recorded on a beach in Lanzarote. What's not to love about it?

1. The Wild Swans – 'Dancing at the Crossroads'

This song is the cream of the crop; there's never been a better one. When we started The 2 Johnnies, our first few gigs were in Wexford, so we quickly learned this song. The place would explode when we played it. It still goes down a treat twenty-four years after Wexford's famous All-Ireland win in '96. And if you're wondering if we attempt to do the rap verse at the end . . . Yes, we do. Although one of these days I'm going to go into cardiac arrest during it.

Honourable mentions

JB: *These classics were unlucky not to make the list, but check 'em out if you get the chance.*

- *'The Mayo Anthem '96'.*
- *Séamus Doran – 'The Mighty Blue and Gold'.*
- *There was a band from Waterford called The Deise Boys who released a cover of 'Brick House' by The Commodores with Lionel Richie but they changed*

the lyric to 'Brick Walsh' after the Stradbally hurler. The YouTube description says, 'The boys do it again with another modern classic. Filmed at the magical Towers of Ballysaggartmore near Lismore.' It's worth a look.

- 'Rock da Déise' by Lamph has the lyrics: 'From every car and every house / the flag was flying high / tonight there's gonna be some session, boi.' Then it goes into a dance version of 'Sweet Child o' Mine'. Them lads are off the wall. I also recommend looking up 'If You Want to Go to Heaven When You Die' – a gas Waterford hurling song.

- Fermanagh have a version of Avicii's 'Wake Me Up' that goes, 'Wake me up when we win Ulster'. And Fr Brian D'Arcy is in the video singing away.

- 'Play It Low into Joe' by the band Yes We Canning is fairly epic and is sung very seriously.

- Another bit of YouTube gold is 'Ooh Aah GAA' by Derry band The Devlins, as performed on RTÉ's Up for the Final (as it was then called) back in 1993.

JB: There are too many more to mention here. Have a trawl around the internet and you'll find some great tunes. Most GAA songs are acoustic guitars and fiddles on songs that sound like The Dubliners with a bit of commentary dubbed over. The videos are usually footage of the band performing to confused children from the local primary school in the county jersey, peppered with snippets of matches robbed from YouTube. I know because I've done it (allegedly).

Always obey the pre-match rituals

JB: *Every county has its own traditions. Seán Treacy, one of the leaders of the Third Tipperary Brigade of the IRA during the War of Independence, was shot on Talbot Street in Dublin in 1920. On the morning of All-Ireland finals in which Tipp play, people from Tipperary, mainly west Tipp, meet at twelve o'clock to remember him at his plaque above the door of 94 Talbot Street.*

Tipp supporters often meet to sing a few songs on the steps of the courthouse in Cork, the night before big games. You could easily commute to Cork for a game, but Tipp are big fans of the night before. Ask any Dublin publican. After a match, the likes of Kilkenny will be straight on the motorway home. Our lads try to get till Wednesday out of it. We once got a lift from a taxi driver into Croke Park and had the usual 'Are ya busy?' chat. He said he wasn't. Monaghan were playing Tyrone, and he reckoned they'd rather walk from the M50 than pay the tenner for a spin. We laughed but didn't believe him until we saw a man in a Monaghan jersey take out his tinfoil pack of sandwiches in the premium section of Croker. He was sitting not 10 yards from a full carvery of roast beef and smoked salmon. I doubt he was much use to the taxi man.

JS: We always like to arrive at a game early and set out our stall for a good day. Pre-game pints are one of the best parts of heading to a GAA match. It's a perfect opportunity to meet up with all your friends and soak in the atmosphere before heading to a big game. Here's a word to the wise: always plan to meet up in a pub that isn't packed to the rafters with opposition supporters.

Trust us, nobody wants to hear 'Limerick, You're a Lady' for four hours non-stop before a game, not even Limerick people. Once you've picked your pub, it's time to settle in for a few pints, have a chat about the game and give your pre-game analysis – a full Ger Loughnane job. Don't spend all your time looking for a seat. We've been going to games for years now and I don't think I've ever got a seat in a pub before a game. They're strictly reserved for the auld boys who've been to every All-Ireland since 1960. They take precedence over some whipper-snapper on the lash. We used to be big fans of getting a hot dog or a burger before the game from a street-food vendor, until someone told us that they don't have any running water, so how do they wash their hands? We've never got to the bottom of this, so if you're a street-food vendor, let us know how you wash your hands. Remember earlier when we said to bring a heap of sandwiches? This is where they come in very handy. Get them into ya. Hungover you will thank you in the morning.

Don't be a spoofer

JB: *There are men who live and breathe hurling and football, and women who know the name of the fella who drove the car for the lad who collected the flags for the south Tipp trials match when Disco Eddie from Killenaule scored his first point for the U14s. Then there'll be someone to dispute their facts with a counterclaim of, 'Well, I was talking to his neighbour's aunt during confession in Clonmel in 1993 and she said that the secretary to the club of the man that washed the jerseys for the team they met in the semi-final said he* didn't score at all.' Proceed with caution. One evening we were talking all things GAA and in walks our mate, saying he might come to the next match with us.

We said, 'Be God, Murph, we didn't know you were into the GAA at all.'

He said, 'Jaysus I know all about it. Shur, me grandfather was on the Waterford team that won the Mick McCarthy.'

Mick McCarthy has fifty-seven caps for the Irish soccer team and has had two spells as manager. The Waterford hurlers have certainly never won him.

We looked at each other.

'Are you sure it wasn't the Dan McGuire he won, Murph?'

He hesitated. 'Oh yeah, could have been.'

'He was probably on the minor team that won the Jerry Maguire, too, was he?'

'I think so. Shur, me ma has all his medals at home.'

We couldn't let it go. 'He must have been on that great team with Don Mullane and Fran Shanahan. Was Paul Hewson and Dave Evans on that team too?'

'All them lads, ya.'

(I doubt it, considering those last two are in U2.)

Smacks said, 'Ah, Murph, I'll leave the hurling to you. I'm more of a soccer man.'

I said, 'Ireland will struggle at the weekend without Tommy Keane.'

Murph says, 'Aw, is he out?'

'Well out,' says we.

We decided there wasn't room for Murph in the car that Sunday.

Sing the national anthem

A bugbear of ours is people not singing the national anthem, and not knowing the words is appalling, as far as we're concerned. It's amazing how people can know every word to an entire Taylor Swift album and not know the words to their own national anthem. Again, loud and proud is our motto here. We're proud Irishmen so we stand and belt out the national anthem; it's a tradition. Even when we were on tour in America, we always made it our business to watch the GAA games. We were blown away when we went to watch a game in a New York pub. When the national anthem played, complete silence fell over the pub and then everybody stood up and sang along. That's what being Irish means, and it's something we'd love to see become the norm here in Ireland.

JB: *During the game when Galway scored a goal, the barman from Tipp pulled the cash register out of the wall in frustration. Can't win 'em all.*

Get back for *The Sunday Game*

JS: After all the excitement from the big game is over and, with a bit of luck, you've got the result you wanted, then it's a race against the clock, trying to get home in time to watch *The Sunday Game*. *The Sunday Game* is an institution in Ireland and has been running for over forty years. It's where everybody watches to see who gets man of the match and what crazy shit the pundits, who sometimes enjoy being pantomime villains, will come up with.

You've got two options when it comes to watching

The Sunday Game. Either be clever and get a bag of chips and head away home and watch it there, safe in the knowledge that you will be as fresh as a daisy for work in the morning, or head to your local for another skinful and make peace with the fact that you're probably going to call your boss in the morning and say that you're sick. Sure they'll understand – they're GAA-mad too. More often than not, we chose the latter option, and we don't recommend it. Then that theme music plays and Des Cahill comes on, which brings an end to another perfect GAA Sunday.

So whether you're belting out 'Eoin Kelly is the son of God!' in the square in Thurles on Munster final day or 'Boolavogue' on your way to Wexford Park for the first round of the Leinster Championship, enjoy it, because nothing beats it. Jesus, writing this chapter has us pumped up. We're heading out to the back yard and recreating Nicky English's famous goal against Cork in Páirc Uí Chaoimh. Deep down we still dream of playing for the county, but for now the back yard will have to do. While we march behind an imaginary Artane Band, you get stuck into this quiz and see if you have what it takes to make it to the top.

Can You Make County?

(answers on page 200)

1. What do the letters GAA stand for?

2. Which moustache enthusiast captained the Wexford hurlers to All-Ireland glory in 1996?

3. He can throw a Marty party wherever he likes!

GAA commentator and Irish sex symbol Marty Morrissey moved from New York City to which county as a kid?

4. Complete his famous quote: 'There won't be _____ _____ _____ in Clare tonight.'

5. Which GAA legend is responsible for the following quote? 'Colin Corkery on the forty-five lets go with the right boot. It's over the bar. This man shouldn't be playing football. He's made an almost Lazarus-like recovery from a heart condition. Lazarus was a great man but he couldn't kick points like Colin Corkery.'

6. As the crow flies, what is the closest establishment to Croke Park in which you can have a pint?

7. Which two-time Offaly All-Ireland-winning hurler allegedly smoked a cigarette in the jacks before an All-Ireland final in Croke Park?

8. Which former Wexford hurler is allegedly quoted as saying, 'If we win another All-Ireland, I'll have to get a second mickey on the road'?

9. Which former Tipperary hurler played an inter-county match in his bare feet?

10. Where in Thurles was the GAA founded? Clue – Smacks passed out here on his graduation night.

11. True or false: Donegal's Jim McGuinness had a perm in the nineties.

12. What is Antrim hurling legend Sambo McNaughton's real name?

13. Who is the only GAA player to win two senior All-Irelands in one year?

14. Who is the only player to win an All Star without playing for even a minute of the championship that season?

15. Who scored the first goal of the millennium in Roscommon's Dr Hyde Park?

How did you score?

0-3/15: You're still only a club player struggling on your senior team. Time to give the weekends in the local a miss and lay off the snack boxes. You're never going to make county at this rate. Time to put in the hard work.

4-7/15: You're on the brink of getting the call-up to the county squad. Everyone in the county reckons you're the next big thing. You've a short distance still to go to get there, though. If you give the group holiday to Santa Ponsa a miss, it might make all the difference and you could be a star. A bit more work and Cyril Farrell could be raving about you on *The Sunday Game* – 'Bang! Over the bar!'

8-10/15: You've arrived on the county panel and are part of the furniture now. You're getting a world of attention in the local nightclub, you're flat out doing appearances at summer camps and you even have a brand deal with a local deli. Can things get any better? You're one step away from being one of the all-time greats, right up there with Páidí Ó Sé, Christy Ring and Johnny Smacks. Greatness awaits you.

11–14/15: Your skills in GAA quizzing are as silky as a 40-yard outside-of-the-boot pass from Mayo legend Ciarán McDonald. Prepare to never pay for a pint again as you're now in the hall of fame. There's a seat at the bar and a frame on the wall in The Boar's Head waiting for you. Enjoy!

15/15: You cheated.

STAGS AND HENS

Stag and hen parties are basically an excuse for fully grown adults to go buck wild and let loose for one weekend. Going on a stag/hen feels like being back in the Gaeltacht. It's an opportunity to leave all your responsibilities behind and forget the real world for a while. We loved talking about stags and hens on the podcast so much that we polled our Instagram followers about them. We realize that our social media followers may not be the best barometer of how to behave, but here are the results anyway.

Should you do an activity while on your stag/hen?

Stag

YES: 53 per cent

NO: 47 per cent

Hen

YES: 58 per cent

NO: 42 per cent

JS: I'm for and against activities. They can help you work up a sweat that goes some way toward killing a hangover. Also, they can be something different and they help the group strike up a bit of camaraderie. But there's a lot to be said for just being drunk for two days. I've been on stags where fellas have paid €30 to *not* play bubble soccer. Christ, one thing they don't tell you about bubble soccer is that it's fairly sore. Several lads have got whiplash, and trying to get up off a timber floor on your knees is an absolute disaster. I got to turn a big lad upside-down, though, which was good craic. He thought he was class breaking everyone else up. But after five minutes of that shite, we were exhausted and decided to play a game of actual soccer instead.

On one stag we went surfing in Lahinch, and the ice-cold Atlantic blew away the hangover. Grand job, but to be honest, I spent most of the time just lying on my back on the surfboard as if I was on a lilo, just contemplating life, wondering would I get fined for throwing up in the B&B the night before. That's what I call a stag! On that stag I also got word that it was imperative that I go home to play in a hurling match for my club, which meant I would have to end my stag experience early. Did I listen to the advice to get an early night? Did I fuck! I went to the nightclub and fell into bed at 1 a.m. Then I was up at six thirty to catch a lift back to Tipp. Pure misery. On the way home I had a bottle of Lucozade and five sausage rolls for breakfast. During the game I bent down to take a 21-yard free, and I'm not proud to admit that I puked up a little. Our selector, Mick, ran in with a bottle of water and said, 'You look like you need this.' He was right. I still scored 1–7 from wing-forward. County. Some punishment. I wouldn't do it now. I was only twenty-three at the time and felt like I was invincible. If I had that breakfast now I'd be sick even with no drink the night before, never mind go and hurl a game on a belly full of Jägerbombs.

I once tried shooting on a stag. It was some pain in the bollox because you couldn't drink. We got thrown out because one of the boys tried to shoot a real crow. Don't get me wrong, we understood that you couldn't drink while handling live ammunition, but still. I did enjoy it for around three minutes. The first couple of shots were a good buzz, but after that I was like, 'Right, where's the bar?' It must have lasted three hours. I could have joined the army after it, a proper SAS job. We eventually arrived at our hotel in Kilkenny at eight o'clock, sober as judges, while other stags were going around dressed as flamingos. They must have thought we were some dry arses.

JB: *I had a similar experience with paintballing. The one time I went, a few of us spent the whole time trying to shoot the only bald lad in the head. The mask covers your face but every time he got shot on his bald patch, he roared in pain. Great day out!*

We hear that a lot of stags are going go-karting as their activity.

JS: That wouldn't do it for me. I have a car with heated seats. How is the go-kart going to be better than that?

JB: *I went go-karting in Galway, which is two hours from home, so obviously we were fairly jarred up from the black and cans on the bus journey. One or two lads stayed sober for the karting, but they were instantly shunned for being no craic. I'm not going to lie, heading out on the track, I was fairly pumped. Having never done it before, I decided I was going to win, and as I pulled out* *of the first chicane I was absolutely lifting. Then I came to a really sharp corner and I was going about 60 per cent too fast and ended upside-down in a row of black silage bales. I didn't win but at least I wasn't deemed no craic. You can recover from losing; you can't recover from being no craic.*

Horse racing is a classic activity that stags have enjoyed over the years. It's a chance to put on suits and lose all your money. A word of advice: do not get too drunk for this one. After a few jars I was ringing everyone I knew, looking for tips.

Trying new things is always a good idea on a stag/hen. We spoke to a female friend of ours who went around the lakes of Killarney on a boat tour for a few hours, drinking and doing karaoke. Right job. The problem was she was seasick and was traumatized for life afterwards. The toilet was out of order and everyone was swollen like calves, getting off the boat. Not ideal.

JB: *Why not try a bit of jiving? It's the perfect activity. I'm definitely in favour of this. Knowing how to jive is an essential life skill down the country and should be taught in schools. I've heard of people getting hired for a job because of their jive performance at a GAA social/wedding. If you go on a stag, it will be all men, so I'm not sure if the jive teacher rounds up a bunch of women, and if so are they young wans or auld wans? Either way is good.*

Should everyone dress in fancy dress on a stag/hen?

YES: 42 per cent

NO: 58 per cent

JS: I'm in favour of fancy dress to a certain degree. It's good craic and can be good to get the buzz going, but it's obviously a nightmare for getting into nightclubs: 'Sorry, lads, not tonight. We don't let Pikachus in the club.' I'm against dressing the stag up in something uncomfortable, though. Trust me, nobody wants to see a sixteen-stone man in a pink thong. Nobody. I want to dress up as members of Boyzone or the squad of Italia 90 for my stag. I'd grow the 'tache and be John Aldridge. I saw one stag dressed up as an air hostess, against his will. He looked like the Joker when he dressed up as a nurse in *The Dark Knight*. After a while he kind of got into it, which was worse. When we got back to town, we went to the GAA club lotto and he picked out the winning ball from the drum, still dressed as a scary air hostess. The Joker bombed a hospital in *The Dark Knight*; I don't know which was worse.

There's a family in town that has a tradition of giving the stag an awful time. They put one fella in his mother's nightdress and waxed him down the back of the bus. It took eight men to hold him down but they had the manpower. They weren't even warming up the wax; they just stuck the strips on like they were Premier League stickers. Slap! Then they ripped them off. They waxed parts of that man that should never be waxed. They drew blood and all. They took the piss on journeys home from the stags, too, these fellas – thirteen hours to get back from Killarney, and we weren't walking. They stopped in Mallow and refused to leave the pub.

Eventually the bus driver stormed in and shouted, 'Get on the bus! Ah, lads, for fuck's sake, it's Mallow.'

They cut the arms and legs off some overalls and put them on another poor groom-to-be. He was like a stripper who was sponsored by John Deere. They didn't do much else to him, just made him wear the overalls all weekend. And that family are my future in-laws. I may have to hire security for my stag.

JB: *We saw a stag in Edinburgh while we were having dinner before one of our gigs over there. The stag himself was bet into a kilt and a ripped England jersey. He'd have been better off naked. I reckon there was definitely nothing under the tartan.*

JS: Lad, tell them all about the time you brought sandwiches on a stag.

JB: *So what? I brought sandwiches on a stag.*

JS: I've been on seven or eight stags and I've never seen anyone bring sandwiches. In a Bag for Life! Bring them on my stag and you're going out the window!

JB: *Yeah, but I get hungry very often and need to eat. On one stag when we'd been drinking all day, the hunger came on me around 9 p.m. and I went for a carvery. The only seat was beside a French tourist. I sat in, not a bother, and proceeded to melt the ear off him for half an hour. I think I knew I was wrecking his head, but he made some comment about culture, and I dug deep into my brain to make the Irish sound civilized. I got tired and reverted to teaching him fake Irish. I said 'Tá tú chomh leithreas' was an ancient blessing you say to friends. It actually means 'you are so toilet,' but, sure, if* *you can't have the craic . . . I enjoyed a nice lamb shank and returned ready for the dancing.*

JS: I went on a stag to Germany for three days and the only thing I ate was a pretzel at four in the morning.

JB: *That's why you felt unwell on the journey home, John.*

JS: True.

Would you rather go on a stag/hen for one night or two nights?

Stag

TWO NIGHTS: 80 per cent

ONE NIGHT: 20 per cent

JB: *The two-night men are the lads you want to hang around with. The fellas who only go for one night are the descendants of people who took the soup.*

JS: There's a sweet spot on that second day when you wake up in a hostel that's a million degrees. You get up, have breakfast and a pint, and your energy levels come back up like a character in Street Fighter, and then you know you can go at it again all day.

The woman who runs a certain hotel in Killarney that I've been to a few times has a great trick. She bursts into your room around nine thirty in the morning and says, 'Well, pet, are ya sick?'

I've had two hours' sleep; of course I'm sick.

'Come down now, pet, and have your breakfast. You've already paid for it,' she says, knowing Irish lads love to get value. She even opens the window.

The first time it happened to me I was like, 'Who the fuck are you? Am I late for work? What's happening?'

She said, 'Come down. You'll feel better for it.'

But she knew that if I got up to eat that breakfast, I'd need cider fast, rapid fast. I walked into the breakfast room and there was a lad singing in the corner. We were off for round 2. We all spent a fortune in there on cider to wash down the kilo of salt she had booby-trapped the sausages with. The woman is a genius. Although I went in there one morning nursing the mother of all hangovers and there was a fella singing 'The Rattlin' Bog'. That was no good. I left immediately. There's never a good time to sing that song.

JB: *The problem with two-day stags is that on the second morning the lads are normally still pissed from the night before. One lad got us barred from The King's Head in Galway at 6 p.m. on day two. He was abusing the band. Later that night I saw him chatting up a woman, and as I walked by, I realized he was showing her something on his phone. It turned out it was a video of Colin Lynch pulling on the Waterford lads during the 1998 Munster final. Smooth operator.*

Hen

TWO NIGHTS: 55 per cent

ONE NIGHT: 45 per cent

JB: *We've obviously never been on a hen. Maybe it's more about the event, the dressing up, matching outfits, blow-up dolls with giant inflatable mickeys. Well, they seem giant to me.*

Painting and prosecco is a thing now. If you said to a fella, 'Do you want to come in and drink a bit of Prosecco while painting some lad who looks like Dermot Gavin naked?' he'd call the cops on you. We don't want to cast aspersions here, but perhaps ladies just aren't into having stout for breakfast while playing pool against a local teenager. Women have reminded us they spend a lot longer getting ready to go out, so the second day is more effort. Lads will shower, put some tar in their hair, dig out the cleanest shirt they can find and go at it again. If we had to stick on eyelashes and wear heels all day, it might be different. Having to straighten your hair and wear an uncomfortable bra is some dose, so we hear.

Ladies, would you be happy for your lad to go to a strip club?

YES: 65 per cent

NO: 35 per cent

JS: No major shock here. Lads have form.

Lads, would you be happy for your missus to go to a strip club?

YES: 66 per cent

NO: 34 per cent

JB: *I have to say I was shocked by this. We see it as just a bit of craic, some dude dressed as a cowboy dancing in front of fired-up women.*

JS: I've seen that film *Magic Mike* about male strippers. If the missus wanted to go, that's fine. I'd be doing some working out though for when she got home! You could grate cheese off Channing Tatum; you could probably roll croissants on me.

JB: *One time in our local pub, a hen brought in a male stripper and the men couldn't believe it. We were all fairly interested to know the craic (not crack). He was dressed as a cop, so the jig was up – guards don't come into country pubs. He sat the hen on a stool and danced around her, taking his clothes off. He went full monty. He was in good nick, in fairness to him, tanned as a Santa Ponsa holiday rep and all oiled up like a rasher. The men were interested in one thing – how much he was getting paid. They were all laughing at him until he said €300 cash, and he was off to Clonmel to do another one. That shut up the mockers. A week's wages for getting your flute out? One auld lad shouted, 'Where do we sign up?'*

One night I found myself playing a gig in Nelly O'Brien's pub in Tipp Town. I can't remember if I had committed a crime and this was my community service or who I slighted in a former life to land myself there, but there I was. We were halfway through 'Black Betty' when in walked this lump of a Polish fella in a black jacket (don't worry, he wasn't the stripper) and he looks around to see if . . . actually, I don't know what he was looking for, because the whole place was full of degenerates. Anyway, he decided the coast was clear and beckoned towards the door. In came a stunning blonde Eastern European woman in a full fake NYPD uniform. Well, the Tipp town boys started shouting and cheering like feeding time at the zoo. It was some header's birthday and his mates had hired the stripper.

She said, 'Where is Mick?' in that thick accent we imagine a Russian spy would have, and Mick was thrown into the middle of the floor. She pulled out a chair and sat Mick on it. She started dancing, and bits of the NYPD gear were flying around the bar. Mick was delighted/mortified and his mates were filming everything (Ballyragget hadn't happened yet). Herself got bored and pulled out a few more stools. Then she grabbed more random lads and they got a dance too. Mick wasn't impressed but he didn't want to make a fuss. Our guitar player saw the last chair empty and sat down on it. The stripper got the baps out – they'd had a few quid spent on them but it was well worth it – and a can of whipped cream came out and not a butterfly bun in sight.

Our guitarist was still playing away, but the stripper didn't fancy 'Black Betty', so we played some sort of blues slow jam that seemed more appropriate for a striptease than The Saw Doctors or 'Come Down from the Mountain, Katie Daly'. She was rubbing off the guitarist while he was soloing away. One of them big nipples nearly had his eye out.

The Tipp town boys were getting too carried away and it looked like they wanted to eat her, so the bouncer decided enough was enough and he threw a jacket over her. She started looking for her bra, but there was a lad on top of the pool table wearing it like a pair of goggles. 'I'm like a bumblebee,' he said, laughing.

'Give me bra,' the stripper ordered as if talking to a bold child.

Most of her props were returned to her, bar a pair of handcuffs, which I saw being used to chain a young *lad to a fence later on. She and her bouncer left and everyone was smiling. It was gas. Then quiet descended and we snapped out of the spell. Four lads had whipped cream on their faces and weren't sure if they were proud of themselves or not. The crowd looked at us. We weren't sure where to go from there . . .*

'Oh come down from the mountain, Katie Daly / Come down from the mountain, Katie, do . . .'

Should you go abroad for a stag/hen?

YES: 59 per cent

NO: 41 per cent

No one knows you abroad, so you can make a show of yourself, not that you'd intend to. You can jump into a fountain in Prague and no one cares. You can do that in Cahir, too, but Councillor Andy will shame you on Facebook.

Dear girlfriends who are reading this book, if your fella goes on a foreign stag, there may be strip clubs.

Sorry, lads, but to the best of our knowledge, there is no strip club in Clonakilty. A friend of ours checked.

If you go foreign, no one can half-arse it. You all have to go for the full thing. No snakes arriving just for the second night.

JS: When I went to Germany, the boys on the bus said you can't get a hangover from German beer as it's got no preservatives. Lying bastards. I drank about twenty pints and lost my phone, and I was as sick as a dog.

We can understand hens and stags heading abroad. It's certainly cheaper. Thirteen quid for a gin and tonic in Dublin, when it's 80 cents somewhere in the world. Going over is great craic. The excitement is in the air as ye tear into a few airport pints. Coming home is heart-breaking. You've a belly full of pints, a brain full of regret and ya can't find your passport. Eventually you board the plane only to find out you're sitting beside some big animal on the Ryanair flight.

Another downside is not knowing the good spots abroad. If you don't know the good places to go in Prague or Bratislava, it can be bleak. The joy of staying local, in somewhere like Killarney, for example, is that someone will know where to go. But in Bratislava, it's not like you've been there for a Munster final before. And you don't want to rely on Trip Advisor, so you ask the taxi driver, but he's got a cousin who runs a club, so he sends you there, but the cousin's club is pure dodge and there's a bang of *Taken 2* off it. You'd want Liam Neeson on speed dial.

Should you bring your other half's parents on your stag/hen?

YES: 53 per cent

NO: 47 per cent

This really depends on age and how well you get along with them. A few drinks in, you might start abusing the life out of each other. Definitely don't bring them on a two-nighter, but how about a nice meal? That's surely handier.

JB: *I can't imagine bringing my father to a strip club. He'd be fixing things and telling them what to do with*

their money: 'Show me that pole, there. Someone'll get a
nasty fall off that. Have ye a Phillips-head screwdriver?'

Is it a bit of craic to have a small lad handcuffed to you?

YES: 37 per cent

NO: 63 per cent

JS: What the hell is wrong with 37 per cent of you? What do you do when you want to go to the jacks? How do you wipe your arse? Ye've been watching too much of *The Wolf of Wall Street*. It's apparently a great night and handy money for the small lads, but I'd rather get Pat Fox handcuffed to me. Now that would be some craic.

Stens

'Stens' – combined stags and hens – are taking off now. We are in strong opposition to this trend, unless ye've had Friday and Saturday to go wild and you meet up for a few on Sunday. That's the only way we would find it acceptable. You're going to spend the rest of your lives together. One weekend apart isn't going to kill you.

JB: *Unfortunately this year Smacks' stag was called off due to the coronavirus. Instead we ended up drinking bottles in his back garden on a damp Sunday. People often ask us to do a video for someone's birthday or wedding, and we do them, but I never saw the appeal, to be honest. When the stag was called off, I contacted Johnny's friends and former GAA coaches and asked* *them to send in a video slagging him. It was the best-spent time we have ever put down. To see Smacks torn apart by his U12 coach because he pulled a dirty tackle playing against a girl fifteen years ago was better than any celebrity shout-out. You can go online and pay Snoop Dogg $500 to say 'happy birthday' and 'wazup!' but he knows nothin' about late nights in Copper's and late pulling in junior hurling, and no one else is going to know about them either, lad. Say not'n! Happy stag!*

WEDDINGS

JS: Weddings normally stem from a romantic proposal, but not mine. After we did a gig in Abu Dhabi, I decided it was the right time to get down on one knee. All I needed to do was get the ring. (It's worth mentioning that rings are tax free in Abu Dhabi, though that's not the main reason I proposed.) So I dragged Johnny B ring shopping. Neither of us is an expert on diamonds, but they were tax-free, so we couldn't go wrong. After getting through airport security, I had the ring in my pocket for safekeeping. Then it all went a bit Pete Tong. We might have overdone it the day before at a pool party – the local barman claimed we set a new record for consuming Corona. As the plane was taking off, I began to feel a bit dizzy and I asked the flight attendant sitting across from me for a glass of water.

He said, 'Sir, we're in transit. We can't leave our seats.'

I said, 'I'm beggin' ya,' and then I slumped in the seat after passing out. Thankfully the seatbelt prevented me from ending up in the middle of the aisle.

JB: *I was fast asleep. I woke up and Smacks looked like he'd been shocked by an electric fence. They dragged him down the aisle of the plane by his ankles. It was hilarious. There was a lad from Kerry on the plane who came up to us when we landed in Dublin Airport and* *said, 'Jaysus, I thought I was after seeing one of The 2 Johnnies die in front of my eyes. That would have been some story.' Then he got a selfie with us.*

The cabin crew asked me Johnny's name and I said, 'Smacks.' The Asian flight attendant kept saying to him, 'Wake up, Mr Smacks.'

JS: I snapped out of it. 'My name's Johnny,' I said, when I woke up with an oxygen mask on me and Johnny B standing over me scratching his head. I was lying on the ground. The staff were stepping over me, trying to sort dinner. I must have drunk four litres of water in ten minutes. All the while I kept my hand in my pocket on the ring.

JB: *I offered to pay to put you in first class but they wouldn't take the deal. You also made me stop filming you. I wish I had kept rolling.*

JS: When I got back to my seat, there was a giant man sitting beside me. They eventually asked him to move so I could have some more room. It was the longest seven hours of my life.

When we landed back in Ireland, it was straight to RTÉ, where we had a studio rented to record a podcast. I got a chicken roll into me as soon as I got off the plane in an effort to revive myself. We drove back to Cahir after the recording and I rang Annie to ask her to order an Indian so we could eat together at home. I had this big romantic proposal planned, but I was so fucked after the trip from hell that any ounce of romance I had left in me went out the window.

As soon as I got home, I threw my suitcase in the front hall and walked up to her father's house to ask his permission. I texted her brother to ask was Annie's father at home and he texted back yes and the ring emoji. Her sister must have leaked my intention to propose (I had asked her for the ring size; women just naturally know these things). I was a bag of nerves, but after my near-death experience on the plane, I had a new sense of determination. When I got to Annie's parents' house, her father was lying back on his bed waiting for me, it was like something out of *The Sopranos*.

I started, 'I'm after getting a ring for Ann Marie.'

He said, 'A what?'

'A ring.'

'For what?'

'For Ann Marie. Is it OK if I ask her to marry me?'

'Oh right. When are you going doing it?'

'I suppose I'll do it now.'

'Jaysus. Right job. I'll be down in five minutes. We'll go into town.'

***

As Annie walked into the sitting room back at our house with the chicken korma and the poppadoms in tow, I was down on one knee. She eventually said yeah. She thought I was messing first but I assured her I was serious.

No sooner had I the ring on the finger than her father and brother burst in the door. We were ordered to get dressed and get ready for town. We had a great night at the Cahir GAA Draw the Joker. I was fair ropey in the Shamrock Lounge – severely dehydrated, room spinning, etc. Everyone was shaking my hand and the sweat was beading out of me, the shirt stuck to my back. People kept buying me whiskey. I don't even like whiskey and the one thing I didn't want to do was drink. The club chairman kept shaking hands with me and announcing our engagement over the speakers during the club draw. We arrived home at two thirty in the morning, sat down and reheated the korma. Some romance!

The next thing we had to do was find a wedding venue. We had obviously never got married before, so we didn't know what we were at. But we knew that there were three main ingredients you need for a great wedding: good music, good craic and free booze. The best wedding I was ever at took place on the west coast of Clare. It had good food, good people, a beautiful view over the ocean, all topped off by the brother of the groom skinny-dipping at four o'clock in the morning. The boys robbed his clothes and he had to walk around the four-star hotel in the nip.

I don't believe in these weddings where you can get a taxi from home. No good. You want to be far away, where you don't know anyone. Well, you know half the crowd, but I mean you need to be free to make a show of yourself in front of the staff and not have to worry about meeting that barman ever again. That's essential.

When we were shopping around for a wedding venue, one place was on our shortlist because we'd done a gig there and really liked the room. We sat down with the wedding coordinator and she offered us each a scone. I don't even like scones but I said I'd have one, out of courtesy. Well, I don't know what she had in it but, Christ, it was incredible. For the first twenty minutes of the conversation, all I could hear was, 'Blah, blah, blah.'

I was just thinking that this is the nicest scone of all time. Jam and cream. Who knew it was so nice? She could have said the wedding would cost €8 million and I'd have just said, 'Yeah, give me another scone.' At the reception our main course will just be scones if I get my way.

When I eventually snapped out of my scone-induced coma, she asked if we had any questions. I asked her, 'When do ye pour the first glass of wine?' It annoys me that sometimes they don't pour until you get your food. If you hear someone complaining about the food, they haven't had enough to drink. My second question was, 'What time does the bar close?' I know a few of my friends don't know when it's time to go home. Third question was, 'What time does the residents' bar close?'

She said, 'I've often seen lads go from the residents' bar to breakfast.'

Then I knew it was my kind of venue.

Picking which finger food to have is a tricky decision. You have to have sandwiches and cake for all the auld wans. They think it's a night out at the bingo. But some older people will go home after the cake. They just need to get their fix of fruit cake and they're away home happy.

JB: *Something that breaks my heart when it comes to the finger food is those goujons that look like chicken but are actually fish. One of the world's greatest deceptions. What kind of monster serves fish goujons? Anyone reading this book will know we love goujons. Throw 'em out, kid!*

One thing to remember when attending a wedding is that you have to be careful at dinner.

JS: Not to get too drunk?

JB: *Not to get too full. I had a bad experience once. The food was lovely and I kept eating and eating. By nine o'clock I couldn't move. Since then I never eat the soup or dessert.*

JS: My approach is to skip dessert and then drink enough so I'm steamed up when the music starts and don't have to leave the floor all night. Might have one when the finger food comes out, but other than that, it's strictly come dancing.

JB: *Going to a wedding nowadays is like heading to Paris Fashion Week. I can't understand women wearing white. There's plenty of other colours to choose from. When I was in a wedding band, I arrived at a wedding around nine o'clock and went up to the bride to ask her how the day was going and if she was ready for a bit of dancing. Sure, she wasn't the bride at all, just some woman wearing white. She must have thought I was trying to chat her up or something.*

Only in the door and all chat with a complete stranger! Well, she shouldn't have worn white. Men aren't getting away scot-free either. Men's suits started getting tight about five or six years ago. The younger guys have the shirts absolutely vacuum-packed onto themselves, and the men over fifty wear shirts that could cover Duffy's circus. Massive.

JS: I've had a fashion disaster at a wedding once. Myself and my friend Choc Ice were trying to do Riverdance at a wedding one night, and during one of my scissor kicks, I split my pants right between the legs. I had to hide in the curtains of the function room until a mate drove me home to get a pair of jeans. A jeans, shirt and tie combo – I was like something out of *Saved by the Bell*. Another one of the lads came in a purple shirt and tie. The boys called him the Joker. True to his new name, by the end of the night, he was face down in the grass outside the hotel. This lad was more of a nuisance than the real Joker.

Another fashion accessory that's been making an appearance lately is the whiskey flask in the suit jacket. There's no way I'm doing that. It throws off the shape of your jacket. My suit will be so tight, you won't fit a credit card in the pocket. Also my missus wouldn't let me drink whiskey before the church. It would probably end up turning into a sing-song.

Dos and Don'ts

Do give a gift

JB: *I'd rather get a summons for court than see a wedding invitation come through the door. You'd get a foreign holiday for the price of attending a wedding. But do give a present.*

JS: We knew a lad who kept saying, 'I have your card in the car.' That was eight years ago and he still hasn't handed it over. Give money. A couple who are dropping twenty grand on a wedding don't want a photo frame; they want hard cash. (If any of my wedding guests are reading this, take the hint.) I know someone who got egg cups. Seriously. Two egg cups with HIS and HERS written on them. If that was my wedding, they wouldn't be getting a main course. I'd give them two boiled eggs. See how they like it.

Do wear a suit

JB: *Who doesn't wear a suit?*

JS: I know a guy who's been to several weddings and not worn a suit. At one he wore a leather jacket, black jeans and a black shirt. He was like The Fonz. At one he actually wore a Guinness T-shirt. Honest to God.

Do settle the nerves the night before

JS: The night before you have to go for a few handy ones. I mean four or five pints in the local – you don't want to be turning up to the church dying, with two red eyes. But you don't want to be at home twiddling your thumbs and getting cold feet either. If you think you're getting cold feet, put on an extra pair of socks and go to the pub. Normally, when the groom arrives, the first couple of hours are spent with all the other married men telling you how shit married life is: 'Oh, it's all going to change now tomorrow,' as if she's going to instantly turn into a vampire. This is a chance for the best man to get out his last few stories about you, ones that can't be broadcast at the actual wedding dinner, while the women from the wedding party are at home fretting and applying nail varnish, or whatever they do while they're wearing matching pyjamas.

Do have something to eat after the church

JS: I'd often stop in for a burger on the way to the hotel.

You could be there by three o'clock and not get your dinner until six or seven. It's a long day from twelve o'clock, when you arrived at the church, and with a few glasses of champagne, or some fruit punch the hotel has inevitably watered down, you could get steamed up fairly quickly. When it's twelve thirty and the DJ is putting on 'Maniac 2000', you'll be thinking, *I'm glad I had that burger.*

Don't be that lad asking for requests off the band and DJ all night

JB: *We have a friend who grew up in Liverpool. He was getting married to a girl from Louth, so the big do was up there. One of our mates from home said to the DJ, 'You know the groom's family are from Liverpool?' and requested the Liverpool FC anthem, 'You'll Never Walk Alone'. The only problem was that the groom is a diehard Everton supporter. The DJ dedicated the song to him and the groom ran the length of the room and had to be pulled off the DJ, who he might have actually murdered if left unchecked.*

Do dance

JB: *Don't be so self-conscious, no one cares. I think it's almost rude to not dance at your friend's wedding. Even if you're cat at it, go out and shuffle around. Make the dance floor look full.*

JS: I want to go through that tunnel that the guests make, all lined up in two rows, dancing like they do at the end of the night. You know when they play 'Leaving on a Jet Plane', except you're not going anywhere, except to the residents' bar. I also want to be carried on lads' shoulders; I love all that. I want the photo with all the hurls too, inter-county job. I'm as good as any of those. I'll stamp on a glass, no bother. Is that Jewish? Doesn't matter, I'll do it. It looks like great craic. Are ya getting all this, Johnny B?

JB: *Yes, groomzilla.*

Do play 'Rock the Boat'

JS: No Irish wedding is complete without 'Rock the Boat'. It's also a chance for a single man to get close to the lady he's chatting to. In a totally respectful way. And it's class craic.

Do put a tie around your head

JS: It's totally acceptable to wrap a tie around the head and rock out to AC/DC with your suit trousers rolled up (particularly difficult in skinny pants). Do it. This is a chance for men who really can't dance to dance.

Don't bring a plus-one you hardly know

JB: *A lady we know brought a lad she'd been scoring on the side. He was a menace. He wanted to fight the mother of the bride and was singing 'Wonderwall' during the speeches.*

Do play a game during the speeches

JS: Some people bet on how long the speeches will go on, or everyone puts a fiver in a glass and it gets passed to the next person every time a speaker says thank you. The problem is whoever wins has to go to the bar and buy a round of shots for the table. It's almost an unwritten rule, and it normally ends up costing you more money if you win.

Don't bother with favours

JS: You know those little gifts the bride and groom leave on the tables for guests? They call them 'favours'. They could be a pot of jam or chutney. What am I going to do with chutney when I'm heading to bed at four thirty in the morning? If you're a bride or groom reading this, remember they are an absolute waste of time and money. There'll be none of that at my wedding, unless I get overruled. Which could happen. Women love them.

Do stay for the day-after session

JS: The day after is basically a chance for the couple to get loose. At the actual wedding I'll have to behave, but the day after I'll be loco down in Acapulco.

JB: *Relatives who have travelled will stay for a while, but by 8 p.m. it should be just the crazy gang, mad for road.*

JS: I don't care who's there. It'll be like another stag. I'm having a party. You need a man with an acoustic guitar. Absolute Sunday tunes – power ballads, like 'To Be With You' by Mr Big. You know, sing-along songs.

JB: *In my wedding band days it was always the big insult. Someone I half-knew would phone me and say they were getting married, let's say on Saturday, 1 June, and then ask, 'Would ye do the Sunday in the pub?' I'd* *say, 'No, we only do weddings.' It's a bit of a slap in the face for wedding bands.*

Do be yourself at the wedding

JS: My mother got up to speak at her wedding, and when I watched the video I swear to God I didn't know who it was. I was like, 'What has happened to my mother's voice?' She sounded like Shania Twain at the start of 'You're Still the One'. I was starting to think she'd had a stroke. She was trying to sound posh, like she had just got a job as a receptionist for KPMG. Some people have a phone voice; hers was like she had just joined the royal family.

Do roast the groom

JS: I saw a best man blow so much smoke up the groom's ass, I nearly got sick. It should be like a comedy roast. I'm here now, entertain me.

JB: *I was best man once and as part of my speech I sang a song I'd written especially for the bride and groom. He was a record producer and massive Irish band Kodaline were also at the wedding. They hopped up on stage and sang 'The One', a song they said they had written for the groom, who they'd known since school. A year later they were in the studio with the groom and said they were going to record the song they had written for him. He said, 'Ah great,' and he started singing my song to them! My song had the bride and groom's names all through it and even a verse about how he really likes computers. Kodaline's song was a bit more relatable for people who weren't there on the day. It went on to sell over 200,000* *copies. I never sang my one again. Easy to mix them up, though, I guess.*

Do go easy on the drink

JB: *I saw a bride fall down the stairs once. She was pretty dinged up but she walked it off. She hadn't eaten because she didn't want to mess up her dress and she had been sipping champagne all day. She was lamped. Old DJs used to tell us that they knew of a few brides who had done the bang-bang with one of her wedding band – on the night of the wedding! I never met anyone who could actually corroborate these stories. I think they're wedding band urban legends.*

The music at your wedding is one of the most important things to get bang on.

If you hire a wedding band, be sound, which means just say hello and make sure they get plenty of goujons. Then the band will put in the effort. Speaking from experience, if the couple are condescending and if there's a lack of breaded chicken, it really impedes the band's performance.

Often a guest would say, 'Can my friend/son/half-dead Uncle Davey get up and sing a song?' Our tactic was to ask them to come back at half-time so we could 'decide what song to play'. It was really a chance to see if Uncle Dave was locked. One family said their cousin had to sing one. He looked at our set list and pointed out a song he knew. I handed him the mic and he turned into Pavarotti. No one had mentioned he was an opera singer. He belted out 'Dancing in the Dark' like it was the requiem from Les Misérables. Another woman said, 'Can my son play a song? He's excellent on guitar.' Again, we

said call back at half-time, and she said, '"Gold".' I said,
'What is?' She said, 'That's the song he knows – "Gold"
by Spandau Ballet, that's the one he knows.' I hid at half-
time. Pure massacre job.

JB: *When we're together at a wedding, which is a rare
occasion, things can get fairly wild fairly quickly. One
time I was playing a wedding that Smacks was at. He
got up on stage and we sang 'The Premier Rap'.*

JS: My missus was mortified.

JB: *Why?*

JS: She knew I was langers. We wouldn't do it now.
Well, not without getting paid. I wasn't supposed to be
drinking as we'd a football match the next day. I turned
up pure ratty and got sent off for elbowing a fella. Eight-
week ban, a nice end to the season. Great wedding all
the same.

JB: *Smacks dared me, saying I wouldn't sing Ricky
Martin's 'Livin' la Vida Loca'. So at half-time the band
and I googled the chords and had it ready to go after
the sandwiches. The hotel had a fella whose job was to
sit beside the dancefloor and ask people not to dance in
their bare feet. If they insisted, he wouldn't do anything;
he'd just make a note of it on a notepad. That was his
entire job. The hotel must have had an insurance claim
or something. After doing it for four hours, he looked like
he'd just returned from war. The eyes were sunk into his
head with boredom. He was definitely not livin' la vida
loca.*

*A good first dance is what gets the whole night going.
I highly recommend letting the band do it. It's a much*

better start than asking the band to use an iPod (the DJ won't be there yet). This means you have to pick a song the band can actually play. If you're booking a band like the one I was in (four or five lads with long hair and beards), then don't ask us to perform an Ellie Goulding track. This happened. Try as I might, I cannot sound like the bould Ellie. Here are my tips for choosing that opening number:

Johnny B's top first-dance songs

- *Jackie Wilson – '(Your Love Keeps Lifting Me) Higher and Higher' (you have to be able to dance, at least a bit)*
- *Hall & Oates – 'You Make My Dreams' (such a happy song)*
- *Bryan Adams – 'Everything I Do (I Do it for You)' (mega cheese but so much fun for the band)*
- *Ed Sheeran – 'Thinking out Loud' (I hate to admit it but it really does work, it's got a nice sentiment and tempo)*
- *Frankie Valli / Andy Williams – 'Can't Take My Eyes off You' (starts romantic and gets to be great craic)*

JB: *When the bridesmaids and groomsmen join in on the first dance is determined by how bad at dancing the couple are. Some couples go and learn a routine and others start looking towards the sideline, hoping to see Liam Sheedy sending in a young fella for the hard yards.*

Lots of people used to have 'Every Breath You Take' by The Police. It's a nice song, but while you're swaying around the floor for your first dance, remember it's actually about a divorce. If you listen to the lyrics, it's pretty nasty stuff. I was once asked to do 'Maniac 2000' as a first dance. We did it too. Great wedding!

JS: If you've ever been to an Irish wedding, you'll definitely have heard these classics. Here are my must-have tunes to get the floor hopping:

Johnny Smacks' top wedding songs

- Van Morrison – 'Bright Side of the Road' and 'Brown Eyed Girl' (Van Morrison is possibly the world's best wedding singer without ever having done a wedding.)

- Simon & Garfunkel – 'Mrs Robinson'

- Queen – 'Crazy Little Thing Called Love'

- Steve Earle (not Ed Sheeran) – 'Galway Girl'

- Anything by The Saw Doctors

JS: And as for the DJ, he's a vital ingredient in a good wedding. I was at a wedding where the DJ announced, 'OK, last song everybody,' and a guest shouted up at him, 'Hey, you little prick, play another one,' and threw a balled-up €50 note at him. He played on. That's the spirit. I've already alerted the DJ who'll be playing my wedding to have these tunes on standby:

DJ set

- **ABBA – any of their songs (they invented weddings)**

- **Kylie – 'The Locomotion'**

- **The Hues Corporation – 'Rock the Boat'**

- Ant & Dec – 'Let's Get Ready to Rhumble'
- Los del Río – 'The Macarena'
- 'An Dreoilín'
- Vengaboys – any of their tunes
- Whigfield – 'Saturday Night'
- Scatman Jon – 'Scatman'
- John Farnham – 'You're the Voice'
- Anything by 5ive
- Neil Diamond – 'Sweet Caroline' (this is where they lift you up on their shoulders)
- Planet Funk – 'Chase the Sun' (the darts song)
- And then finish with 'Maniac 2000' by Mark McCabe

Our listeners send us in loads of correspondence each week to The 2 Johnnies Podcast. Here are two of our favourites, which should give you food for thought when it comes to planning your big day.

I used to work in a bar in a hotel and I've only seen a free bar for a wedding once. The father of the bride was paying for it. I think there were 200 or so people there. He told us to stop at €10,000, which they reached at midnight, so he just let it roll on. I think it was €13,000 overall. But the worst problem was people taking the piss, asking for doubles all the time, top-shelf whiskeys and so on, and if we were down stock – let's say there are twenty shots of vodka we couldn't account for from the week before – our manager told us to just put twenty down on the free bar. That's the real annoying bit.

As for a drinks reception, I don't think I'd have one because every single person gets shafted at it – shite prosecco for an outrageous price. And definitely not a cocktail reception – we had to serve sixty mojitos and daiquiris, which should amount to three-and-a-half bottles of Bacardi. We were told to use one. Maybe that was just the hotel I worked in. If you use this, keep me anonymous because I'll be battered. If you want the name of the hotel, I'll tell you. The general manager is only a prick anyway.

— Anonymous, Cavan

***

A couple of years ago, my buddy Stephen asked if I'd be his best man for his wedding, and by consequence deliver the best man's speech after the meal. To say I was apprehensive during the meal would be an understatement. Filled with nerves after the main course, and after slowly filling myself with a cocktail of rosé, prosecco and pints of Guinness, I decided to strain the spuds. Whilst I stood at the urinal, rehearsing the imminent best man's speech in my noggin, a young gentleman I had never seen before arrived alongside and pulled out his lad for a wee. After explaining he was a springer spaniel breeder, and a second cousin of the bride – twice removed, from her Uncle Micky's side of the family – he asked how I was fixed for my forthcoming speech. I explained my nerves, and after zipping the flute back into his trousers, he produced a small zip lock bag from the inner pocket of his suit jacket. He told me it was Xanax and placed two in my hand. Upon inspection of the tablets I saw the expiry date was for Christmas 1999, almost a decade in the past. He advised me to take no notice of the date and that like a tin of beans, the tablets improved for ageing. Besides, he assured me, 1999 was a great vintage for Xanax.

So during the dessert course, I washed the two tablets down with a sup of Smithwick's, and within the hour I was feeling pretty damn GROOVY. With a smile from ear to ear, my anxiety and apprehension had long been resolved, and so on to making my speech. Up I stood, confident, projecting my voice into the room, making eye contact with the key players of the day – mothers, fathers, the bride and groom. I had them in the palm of my hand – with the room roaring laughing, clapping, and finishing with a standing ovation.

Unfortunately what happened in reality was less Colin Firth in The King's Speech *and more Leonardo DiCaprio in* The Wolf of Wall Street. *And I am referring to the scene where he drags himself out of the country club and into his Lamborghini after a trip on Quaaludes gone wrong. The photographer's photos from the day paint a truer picture of my speech. There I was in the centre of the function room – writhing around on the floor like a slug, foaming at the mouth, talking and laughing to myself, before being lifted off the ground and brought to the hotel's on-site first-aider. I've not been asked to make a best man's speech since, nor have I kept in touch with Martin, the bride's second cousin.*

Anyway, sure look, sure listen, you can't win them all. All the very best.

— Nate, Dublin

ORGANIZING A LOCAL GAA FUNDRAISER

JB: *I picked up my shopping basket and made for the fruit and veg. Coming towards me is Johnny Smacks, patrolling the aisle like John Wayne playing the sheriff, but dressed as a butcher. A long way from the meat counter, he was definitely dossing.*

'I'm told I'm in charge of this fundraiser,' he says.

'Congratulations,' says I.

'You'll come in and give a hand. You know about microphones and that stuff,' says Smacks.

Just like that, we were up and running, co-chairmen on a GAA subcommittee. Fellas get less for murder. As the event drew closer, the question of an MC arose.

'We'll do it ourselves,' we say.

There was a long silence in the meeting room.

'Anyway, we're free of charge.'

That seemed to win them over. This was long before The 2 Johnnies, when our only appearance on stage together had been a half-rehearsed cameo in the Cahir pantomime production of Robin Hood. We spent five minutes slagging Prince John, who wasn't even in this version (we'd neglected to read the script). This time things would be different.

We decided to hold a *Strictly Come Dancing* night, like the television show, but we wouldn't be keeping it strictly ballroom, as a few of our contestants said all they could do was 'a bit of a jive' and that's what they were going to do, regardless. The club was confident it would draw a massive crowd, so no pressure, then. They've also been confident we'd win the South Championship every January for the past ten years and there's no sign of a trophy yet. This had to work – we had zero experience, so what could go wrong?

JS: From day dot, I've always said you need to look the part, because even if you're shit, at least you've got that going on. That's always been my approach to life. Anyway, all MCs wear suits. I'd seen Dermot O'Leary wear one on *The X Factor* and he looked class, so we'd wear suits. There's only one menswear shop in Cahir, run by a GAA fanatic, our mate Val. He gave us a loan of matching suits. I'll never forget it, they were grey, matched with white shirts and black shoes. We were already the best-looking people in the room.

Deckey the DJ used to play 'Let's Get Ready to Rhumble' by Ant & Dec in our local pub, and the Choc Ice and I used to try to do the dance to it round The Gate House bar. When Johnny B and I decided we'd open the show with a musical number . . . well, it wasn't going to be 'The Locomotion' (another epic tune, to be fair). We learned off the dance routine properly in the spare bedroom and changed the lyrics to be about the contestants. 'Stephan and Shauna, Hughie and Áine, Barry and Orla, we can't name all of ya / Let's get ready to rhumble.' We danced like lunatics. It went down a treat, we think. But we can't be sure, as the crowd were fairly stunned. They probably thought we were tossers.

We must have had seventy cue cards in our hands. We had scripted almost every word we were going to say, strutting about with our wireless microphones. The fact that I'm deluded really stood to us. Anyone else would say, 'Ah, we'll have a bit of craic. Be grand.' We went all out. We started the second half with a rendition of 'Footloose', for no reason except we'd sung it at a local twenty-first one night in The Hill Inn, scuttered. I didn't even know there was a twenty-first on. We were balloobas.

Cahir people are wonderful. They're always ready to think, *Ah, there's just something wrong with them two lads.* They've never once judged us for going around like we were Ant & Dec (that we know of), on stage singing, 'I'm Smacks / I'm B / A duo, a twosome / So many lyrics we're frightened to use 'em.'

We signed off the night by saying, 'Thank you very much. We'll see you at the front bar for live music by Maureen.' At ten to six in the morning, the barman was trying his best to close the bar. The local sergeant looked at him sternly and said, 'One more round.' Overall the event had the desired effect: the club raised a fortune and we got a career. Everyone's a winner.

JB: *Monday morning we returned to work, a bit tired and fairly hungover. Something had changed, though. We'd been dazzled by the lights of the stage, and we both knew we'd never be the same again. One of the participants, Martin, who had danced a lovely Viennese waltz, bumped into us that evening. He said, 'I don't* *know what it is, lads, but ye've got something.' Thanks, Martin. We don't know what it is either.*

JS: That was just the first of many fundraisers we'd find ourselves involved in. Wexford's Fittest Superstar was particularly weird. It was basically like *Ireland's Fittest Family* but in a function room. I only did it because I was promised a lot of free drink and a free room by Wexford captain Matthew O'Hanlon.

Davy Fitz was running the event, and it was the first time I'd met him. He asked, 'Everything OK with your room, ya?'

I was too afraid to tell him they hadn't even got me a room. I ended up sharing a bed with two members of the panel. I also ended up wearing the ear off Davy for about an hour in The Stores.

Anyway, we were only back from America (two weeks of eating quarter-pounders), and the last thing I needed was that mad bastard shouting in my face. 'Come on, Johnny, pump the legs, you have it in ya!' I had three pints of Lucozade in me. But again deluded me thought, *I might go and win Wexford's Fittest Superstar.*

I was supposed to be the celebrity draw, but I could see kids dying inside, watching me almost pass out from angina on the hang tough, a bar 8 ft off the ground that you have to hold on to using your upper-body and core strength. I didn't have much of either. I still held on for a minute, Lee Chin only lasted a minute and fifteen seconds, and he's an inter-county superstar. We also had to do a solid minute of box jumps, again with Davy shouting at me the whole way through. No wonder lads would go through a wall for him. But I wasn't one of those lads. I was thinking, *I'm not gonna exhaust myself doing this. I'm going out tonight.*

I wasn't at my fittest, obviously, but on my team was a Wexford player who was only back from injury and had a point to prove. The papers had said he wasn't fit. The worst round was the Eliminator, like the one on the TV show *Gladiators*. It was a mad obstacle course designed to break hearts. When one of our teammates was having trouble scaling the 10 ft wall, this Wexford player grabbed her by the hips and horsed her over. I'd say she got some hop on the other side. He threw a sandbag at one stage and nearly broke a lad's leg. He had a look in his eye that said he'd rather die than lose this obstacle course.

We still lost. I was delighted. The earlier we got knocked out, the earlier I got to the bar. In the end I did have to pay for my own drink. I'm not calling ye out, Wexford County Board.

Davy gave me a handshake on the way out.

'Thanks for that,' I said. 'Thanks for the hospitality.' He's still Davy Fitz. What was I going to say?

JB: *It's hard to choose what fundraiser your club should hold. Years ago someone in our club had the idea that we'd make a giant sausage and push it the length of the county in conjunction with Irish Guide Dogs to (somehow) raise money. The sausage was sponsored by some meat company, but it was made out of Wavin pipe and plastic wrap on an Ifor Williams trailer. The 25 ft plastic sausage was on top of a bale and was being pushed from Cork to Dublin. But I clearly remember us pulling up outside the roundabout in Clonmel, letting* *a few young lads push the trailer which held up the gigantic sausage through town, then turning around, pushing it back through town again, hitching it back onto the car and driving to Cashel. It was for a good cause. All bets were off.*

A big winner nowadays is local clubs running their own gigs. In essence you hire in a band – say, Aslan – pay them and charge everyone else a fortune for tickets. There's no law down the country – allegedly – so you can serve all night and serve who you like. It's not like in a pub where you have to say, 'Oh, you've had enough.' If you have money, you're on the ball. The age restrictions are a bit fuzzy too. No one has been asked for ID in Knockavilla since the War of Independence. Dan Breen was the last man to be carded out there. Bagatelle are sure to be there, too. They must have played every small festival and fundraiser in Ireland. We're fairly sure they've put on their own gigs and just called them festivals.

JS: My hometown of Roscrea tried something like this, too. They ran a Lark in the Park. It was rumoured that the act was going to be Mickey Joe Harte and that he was hotter than fresh tea. Everyone was buzzing. At the time the town was hosting the Saudi Arabian Special Olympics team and they were the guests of honour at the fundraiser.

The MC announced over the mic, 'And now for the enjoyment of the Saudi Special Olympics team . . . Brian Ormond!'

'Ah, fuck this!' I shouted.

Turns out Mickey Joe was playing in Nenagh.

Instead we were stuck with Brian Ormond singing Boyzone covers all night.

JB: *Not to be outdone, my band were playing at a Cahir fundraising gig, when we were interrupted in the middle of our set because the MC was going to interview a former Ireland footballer. The committee were quite excited, and the MC reminded us of how important this was to raise the profile of the festival. When the footballer came out, we had no idea who he was. We were starting to think he was just having the committee on, pretending to be a footballer from the seventies.*

The small festival is becoming a hot money-making solution. A local committee sees another club run one and the attitude is, *Jaysus, if they can do it, we can.* Everyone wants to hold one. Every year, Holycross in mid-Tipp puts on a country music festival that attracts 10,000 mad bastards in cowboy hats, all spending money.

Another Tipp club told us they were looking into running one, so they asked the only man in the parish who knew about music to get the acts. 'How about a DJ?' the chairman inquired.

'Oh, I don't think that's the type of crowd you want to attract,' said your man. 'Them lads would be bouncing off the walls, taking pingers and all that.'

Like he was thinking maybe DJ Francis from town, or someone to warm up the crowd. He didn't mean Basshunter (although he'd probably do it).

In our experience the best fundraiser is a local *Strictly Come Dancing*. It's a guaranteed winner. For some reason Irish people love dancing. Now prepare to be astounded, because we're going to let you in on some secrets to hosting a fundraiser show that will make your club a bag of cash. Follow these six steps to success and you can't go wrong.

How to Run a Local Fundraiser

Step 1 – Form a committee

There's a reason this is number one on the list. No man is an island, or no two men in our case. It's important to listen to other people, and they'll come in very, very handy when you have to delegate jobs that you don't want to do. Also, when it comes to picking the committee, you have to pick people you like and who are a bit of craic. There's nothing as bad as heading to a meeting after a twelve-hour shift only to sit for three hours listening to someone waffle on about their bunions or how overgrown the weeds in the back yard are . . . or maybe that's just our club. (I hope people from our club don't read this book or we will have to watch our backs.)

You have to get a good blend of youth and experience. The young people will be full of brand-new ideas and they'll be enthusiastic to make the event a big success. When picking experienced members of the committee we always advise picking a farmer or two. Why? Because they love hard work. When we selected our committee, we made sure to pick our club chairman. He was a farmer who dipped sheep, dosed cattle and milked cows, all while holding down a full-time job as a lecturer. Lending a hand in a local Strictly Come Dancing fundraiser would be a cakewalk to this man. For some strange reason he also had the phone number of everyone in town, and to this day we don't know why, but it came in handy. He also had this unbelievable knack of making people do things they didn't want to do. The man was extremely persuasive, thanks to pure farmer determination. It was as if he was a magician. Before you knew it, you'd agreed to clean out his jeep and you were none the wiser. Whenever he made a statement or said anything at a meeting, he would finish by banging twice on the table. This seemed to give his point more weight, so no one ever questioned him or answered back. Genius.

Once your committee is sorted it's on to the next step.

Step 2 – Prepare to spend a few pound

You only get one chance at putting on a good show, so you've got to spend a few pound to give people value for money. What you don't want to happen is to be charging €20 a ticket and then on the night a load of people start going bananas because they can't see or hear anything. Get a good stage, good lights and someone who knows what they're doing to operate the equipment – a professional, if you will, not just an electrician who once played in a cover band. We've seen it happen.

When we first approached our GAA committee with the idea to hold a fundraiser, they were all for it – anything to bring in a few pound to get the kids new jerseys. Their minds then went into overdrive: 'Jeez, we could build a new stand, maybe even an AstroTurf pitch.' We had to bring them back down to earth to remind them that we were putting on a Strictly Come Dancing night in the local hotel, not Live Aid in Wembley.

All was going well until we told them we'd need a few grand to put on the event. We didn't get the reaction we expected; you'd swear we shot someone. We glanced over at the club treasurer; it was up to him to make the call. We thought we'd have to run for the nearest defibrillator for him. He almost turned green and his eyes were bulging out of his head like a cartoon character. It was like a scene from *The Mask*, you know the one with Jim Carrey, where his eyes jump out a foot from his head. We in turn felt like we were making a pitch on *Dragons' Den*. Although, unlike *Dragons' Den*, this idea wasn't going to make us any money. It was all for the love of the club and the fact that we wanted a decent hot shower after a match. Eventually, after some round-table discussions that would give the United Nations a run for its money, our budget got the green light and we got to work on the show.

Step 3 – Pick the right contestants

Finding local people to get on stage and prance around in front of half the town – and essentially make a show of themselves – is not easy. Ideally what do you want is a load of popular figures from your town. You know what we mean – the fella who ties the tie around his head at a wedding and dances to AC/DC for two hours non-stop, he'll do. Or that lovely woman who works in your local bar; sure, wasn't her cousin a Billie

Barry kid? Surely she can dance? She'll be ideal.

Again our club chairman came to the fore here with one of his genius ideas. He proposed that we pick one member from each of the biggest families in town to compete. Initially we were stumped and couldn't understand what he was up to, but he assured us there was method to his madness. He said that by picking from the biggest families, you increase ticket sales. He explained, 'I'm telling you now, if you pick one of the O'Gormans, sure, there's around twelve of them, and they'll all want to see the young one making a show of herself. Sure, that's twenty-four tickets sold straight away. And I'll tell you another thing: there's four or five more families in the parish that are as good as them to breed. We will get on to them, too, and we will be sold out.' He wasn't wrong.

Step 4 – Treat the contestants well

It's very important not to treat the contestants as just pieces of meat who are there to earn the club a quick bob. You're a community organization, after all. As well as getting them to perform in the fundraiser, you also want them to become part of the club if they aren't already. Looking after the contestants is like managing a soccer team; some team members have different requirements than others. For example, we had managed to convince one of the most popular young fellas in Cahir to take part in the Strictly Come Dancing. Shane was well known around the pubs in the town and everyone loved him. Now, he had some requirements that we had to take into consideration. We had to do a deal with him to get him on side in the first place; he insisted we put him with the best-looking woman taking part. Consider it done, we said. He was our marquee signing and we had to keep him happy.

We also enlisted the help of a professional dance teacher to whip the participants into shape. She was a tough woman but we had to let her in on our plan to keep our marquee signing sweet. At the first rehearsal, after the dance teacher had given a twenty-five-minute sermon on how no alcohol was to be drunk at practice, our VIP contestant, Shane, strolls in the double doors of the hall with a large bottle of cider in each hand, completely unaware he was thirty minutes late. We all turned a blind eye. That's our definition of treating a contestant well. Was it worth it? All in all, Shane was responsible for around a hundred ticket sales at €20 a pop. You're damn right we were right.

Step 5 – Get a good MC

Most clubs' criteria for being the host of a show is that said person has held a microphone once before, or that they're an auctioneer at the local mart: 'Right, he can clearly talk. That's good enough for us.' Never a good idea. You've got to have an MC who's got charisma and can carry off the show but who at the same time doesn't make everything about them. Although that sounds rich coming from two fellas who dressed up in matching suits for their first show in public.

In 2015 we were judges at a Stars in Their Eyes event for a local club in Tipperary, where we witnessed the MC raffle off a hairdryer for twenty-five minutes in between acts, for absolutely no apparent reason.

He thought it was hilarious. Everyone else was bored silly. We heard one lad from the third row shout, 'Get on with it, ya prick.' For once we agreed with a heckler.

Another time we managed to get ourselves selected as judges for Lattin's Got Talent. How prestigious. Did it have talent? We'll let you decide that one, although it is the birthplace of Nicky English, so they can do no wrong in our eyes. To host the event, they had employed the services of a local man who reckoned he was the next Bruce Forsyth or Mike Murphy. His only problem was that he wasn't great with names. But surely he couldn't go wrong with The 2 Johnnies? The name pretty much explains itself.

JS: Wrong. He could. If I recall correctly, the first act was two sweet OAPs doing their impression of Johnny Cash and June Carter's hit song 'Jackson' (I don't think it was meant to be comedy, but we just couldn't stop laughing).

After the performance, the host came to the judges for some comments. 'OK, we'll start with yourself, one half of The 2 Johnnies – Tommy Snacks,' he said. I kid you not. Unbelievable! For the rest of the evening any time he came to us we would call him by a different name: Willy, Seán, Peter, Cornelius, we called him every name under the sun. These events are loose, but it's for a good cause, so keep the show going even if sometimes you just have to make your own fun.

Step 6 – Enjoy yourself

Just don't enjoy yourself *too* much. You've all probably heard of 'the Strictly curse', a term coined by the British media. It's used to describe a scenario when people who appear on the BBC's *Strictly Come Dancing* end up cheating on their partners and leaving them for their *Strictly* dance partner. It sounds like something that only happens in movies or on TV, but trust us, it happens a lot closer to home than that. In the early days of The 2 Johnnies, we hosted a lot of local events to gain experience and learn our craft. We were once booked by a club to MC a local Strictly fundraiser. Two weeks before the event, the club chairman called to say that the event had been called off. We weren't too bothered as it meant we had a rare Saturday night off, but we were curious to know what had happened. The chairman said, 'Come here, boy, and I'll tell you now. They're all gone haywire down here. They're like dogs in heat. There's more riding going on than at the Galway Races.' Turns out three marriages were on the rocks following the rehearsals. Always remember that if you're taking part, you're there to raise a few quid for the club; you're not Julia Roberts and the local butcher most definitely isn't Richard Gere, so keep it in the pants and enjoy the experience.

When we speak to people who've taken part in this type of fundraiser, they have nothing but good things to say. So if you're reading this and you're on the fence about taking part in something similar, our advice is to go for it. You won't regret it. It's good to take a trip outside your comfort zone every once in a while, and if it does go tits up you can at least fall back on the fact you did it for charity.

Most of the fundraisers we've been involved in or attended are fairly straightforward affairs. That's not to say there aren't some crazy ones out there. Here are some of the craziest fundraisers we've ever heard of and some ideas you can take inspiration from:

- Turloughmore Hurling Club holds the record in Galway, with six county titles in a row. They have another notable achievement, though. In 1988 they buried a man alive. Team captain and All-Ireland winner Frank Burke got into a coffin and was buried six feet under for two nights. It was to raise funds for new club and community facilities. When asked how he would pass the time, Frank said, 'I don't think my relatives are talking to me, but hopefully my friends will call down and occupy my time via the telephone. I have the Galway GAA annual too. That will be interesting. I haven't taken anything in the way of food down with me, but hopefully a leg of chicken or a sandwich will appear down the pipe.' When asked how he was going to ring in the New Year, he said, 'I haven't any plans but maybe someone will drop a baby Powers down the pipe to me.'

NOTE: The world record for being buried alive was once held by Tipperary man Mike Meaney. The Ballyporeen barman was buried in a coffin for sixty-one days in 1968. Not as a fundraiser, just for the craic.

- Mayo county hurler Cathal Freeman successfully ran a marathon distance of 42 km around a 30-metre loop of his garden while soloing a sliotar, raising over €50,000 for the Irish Cancer Society and PPE for HSE staff. The 29-year-old completed the task on 6 April 2020, having never run more than 10 km before.

- During lockdown loads of clubs got involved in internet challenges. One popular one was to get people to run 5 km, post their time on social media, donate a few bob and nominate more people to do it. The lads stayed fit and the few pound was raised – happy days. Once everyone in a neighbouring club to us had run a few miles and completed the other popular challenges, they started the Drink a Raw Egg Challenge. The sooner they got out of lockdown the better. They went mad in isolation.

- Kildorrery GAA in County Cork held a club draw in 2017. With prizes like these on offer, it's no wonder they made a fortune:

  - Third prize: 1 tonne of animal feed

  - Second prize: Pedigree Vendéen sheep

  - First prize: Pedigree Limousin heifer

- In 2015, Park/Ratheniska GAA in Laois raffled off a shed. You'd be thinking, *Well, I don't need a giant industrial shed*, but if the ticket was only a fiver, sure, you'd have a go. It was won in the end by a Kerryman. Are you surprised?

- Carrickedmond club in Longford held a Calves to Cash campaign, where local farmers were encouraged to rear an extra calf that would eventually be sold on, with the proceeds going to the club. A local business sponsored the milk replacer to rear the calves, and they were hoping the prices for two-year-olds would be in the region of €1,200 each. They started with fifteen calves. The parish priest was one of the first to put his hand in his pocket and buy a calf. What he did with it we don't know. Maybe he ate it, or maybe it's still roaming the garden of the parochial house.

- One of our personal favourites is Pick a Poo. Divide the pitch into squares, sell the squares for as much as you can get, then let a cow into the field. Whoever owns the square the cow shits in, wins the prize. We saw a club use a bull once. It did not go well. The bull went buck wild in the goalmouth and wrecked the shagging thing.

- Cuala GAA in Dublin ran Dalkey Dating, where you could bid money to get a date with some of the players. We don't know how much they raised, and we're not knocking our club, but we'd say our junior hurling team wouldn't raise the price of the post-game box of bananas.

- Our own town has had a few great ones, like the time the publicans played the guards in a game of Aussie rules. Someone got fifteen singlets and a small rugby ball and off they went, hell for leather in a game that saw several late challenges against the cops (perhaps a bit of revenge for stopping late opening). The publicans claimed the win – it wouldn't be like the guards to break the rules – and a great time was had by all. That was the nineties – a different time. In 1990 Cahir ran a telethon, raising money for People in Need. Out of all the blockbuster movies in the world, they chose to reenact a scene from *My Left Foot*, the 1989 Oscar-winning biopic about Christy Brown, a Dublin man born with cerebral palsy who could only use his left foot. Members of the GAA club and other townsfolk acted out a scene where the local kids wheel Christy down the main street of Cahir in a wheelbarrow and tip him out on the ground in the middle of the town square so he can play in goal for a game of soccer. A local man played the part of Christy with conviction, never once breaking character, complete with facial expressions and body movements. There was a penalty, and someone shouted the famous line, 'Let Christy take it!' The other actors, who appeared to be the Cahir U14 team, carried local Christy a few yards, threw him back on the road and he booted it into the top corner. If you have nine minutes and fifty-eight seconds to spare, we recommend you watch this incredible production on YouTube, because it won't be recreated again.

After reading this chapter, your GAA club should have a hot tub, because you now have the tools to go out into the world and raise lots of cash.

We're hoping our GAA club will let us use their field to host our own festival: Cans in a Field. We're in talks with country superstar Jimmy Buckley, and Daniel O'Donnell is going to do a DJ set.

We've got so many great memories from fundraisers over the years. Shout-out to our local publican Hughie, who is now famous for being the proprietor of the Shamrock Lounge, thanks to *Noel's*

News. When Hughie took part in our Strictly Come Dancing, he had a bigger rider than Liam Gallagher – a motorbike! We'll never forget the sight of six lads trying to push a Triumph Tiger Explorer 1200 up a scaffolding plank to get it into the venue. There was nearly a massacre. In the end they settled for a Honda 125. It did the job. Hughie only sat on it for five seconds at the start of his performance. The Chairman of the juvenile club nearly had a hernia loading it every night. But the next time we went into the Shamrock, Hughie gave us two dinners on the house for sorting it. Vroom, vroom, Hughie!

The standout contestant from all of our GAA fundraisers was a mechanic from out the country. When he came up and introduced himself, we honestly couldn't understand a word he said. The man needed live subtitles. He was carrying a pint of Carlsberg like a gunslinger, spilling as much as he drank. He told us he was going to sing Meatloaf's 'I'd Do Anything for Love' at the Stars in Their Eyes event we were organising. He insisted on the seven-minute version because 'that's the one I have in the van'. We had to edit the track, but he pushed us to keep the 'good long intro'. When he took to the stage, we were a little nervous, to say the least. The song didn't play, and we looked at the sound man. He was frantically pressing buttons. Meanwhile, Meatloaf was on stage in complete silence. He started tapping the microphone . . . dum dum . . . dum dum . . . like a heartbeat, as he calmly stared into the crowd. You could hear a pin drop, and people didn't know what to expect.

Eventually the motorbike sound effects and piano kicked in. He began, 'And I would do anything for love . . .' What came out of his mouth was the greatest tenor voice we'd ever heard. He was better at singing Meatloaf than Meatloaf. He brought the house down and won the whole competition. That night at 4 a.m. in the residents' bar he sang 'Two Out of Three Ain't Bad' like a B-side to his earlier performance. He still had the Meatloaf shirt on him and, Christ, it was manky. His frills were in his pint of Carlsberg at one stage. What a performer, though. We haven't heard him sing since, but if he's half as good a mechanic as he is a vocalist, there won't be a car broken down in town again.

Now we're wrecked from writing, so we're heading for a lie down. You go off and organize a fundraiser for your club (when Covid fucks off) and let us know how you get on. We manage a Meatloaf tribute act if you're interested.

THE BOOM

JB: *By eleven thirty people are starting to ask the question: 'Are ya going above?' Everyone knows the answer; everyone's going. Knock back the rest of your drink, say 'I might see ya inside' to whoever or whatever you're trying to chat up, and make a bust for the door. A short walk up the hill, try to straighten up walking past the bouncers, hand in your coat and pay your tenner to get it. It's not Ibiza or Manhattan. This is our small town, and we have a nightclub (well, a large room on the side of the hotel). Over the door is a drum kit with skins signed by U2. There are disco balls hanging from the ceiling and spray paint on the walls. The music is loud enough to be heard in Algeria. There are two bars, and one of them only sells cans – 500 ml cans of Budweiser or Bulmers, that's the drinks list. The other bar has a special on Fat Frogs. The queue is four deep. Fifty-euro notes are waved in the air in an effort to catch the barman's eye. When fellas finally get to the bar, they buy enough alcohol to eradicate the coronavirus.*

Through the dried ice and flashing lights, you can tell everyone is well dressed. Well, not well dressed but expensively dressed. Collared shirts with patterns on the cuffs that people only see because you show them, Lee Cooper jeans bought for €90 that morning in Clonmel, brown Wrangler shoes that will be destroyed by lads standing on them. And the sticky floor is like a Soviet chemical weapon. It doesn't matter; fellas will buy a new pair for next weekend.

A fella beside me at the bar points and asks the barman, 'What's that fancy-looking bottle of stuff?'

The barman is some student who doesn't care if the place burns down. 'Tequila Rose,' he answers.

'Gimme wan of them,' growls my man. 'Johnny B will have wan too.'

I had just drunk two Fat Frogs and had more sugar in me than Willy Wonka's factory. 'That's the job,' I say.

We drink them. They're stink.

'Excellent!' my friend exclaims. 'We'll have two more.'

I try to escape, and he buys more horrendous Mexican liquor for half the town. He's nineteen and an apprentice plumber. To say money is flush is an understatement. The bank phoned him earlier to inform him he qualifies for a twenty-grand car loan. 'No way,' he tells me. 'I'm not a fool.'

By this stage the nightclub is absolutely lifting. Buses bring in punters from nearby villages, hyped up on Heineken, vodka and maybe more. But they're mostly just buzzing from not having a care in the world. Ireland is on one giant stag. When the bar starts to close, the shutters come halfway down and lads start to panic and frantically wave cash, trying to get served one more time. No point walking home sober, I suppose. We all pour out onto Castle Street, many not stopping to collect their jackets. The street is like Mardi Gras meets the Fleadh Cheoil: people singing, some girl crying and her friend saying, 'He's not worth it.' There's a fight, of course. If you take lads who couldn't navigate school, put them on a building site and give them €1,000 a week, don't be surprised when they explode all weekend. There's one Polish lad who can do roundhouse kicks. He's to be avoided. But other than that, hurl away. The guards have a track worn from bringing lads up to the drunk tank.

Next door to the nightclub, an old FCA building has been converted into a Supermac's. Trying to get served in that place is like trying to get into a lifeboat on the Titanic; young and old are cutting each other's throats for a curry chip. It doesn't matter who you are or how many houses you've just bought, the queue for the chipper is the great leveller. They have two bouncers, and you better believe they're earning their pay. To the right of me, a man in a Superdry jacket is leaning over the counter, trying to explain that he wants no taco sauce on his taco chips. His mates grab him by the legs and tip him head first over the counter. No one bats an eyelid.

The stressed-out night manager is from Lithuania and I'd say she's reconsidering her move to Ireland, but she keeps the snack boxes (a staple of the Irish diet during the Boom, up there with breakfast rolls and 100 per cent mortgages) coming. The diving man has regained his place in the queue, and beyond him some lad is punching the arcade machine in the corner, one of those ones with a big claw that pulls out cuddly toys. As usual the SpongeBob falls from the claw just a second before it reaches the hatch. Your man loses the rag: 'Where's me SpongeBob, ya prick?' The bouncers explain that he can't have SpongeBob as they escort him out the door. Somehow this man has friends and *they are getting involved now: 'Ah, he's only having the craic. Give him out the auld SpongeBob.' A royal rumble breaks out, all over a fluffy toy.*

The guards pull up outside in a hurry and run into the chipper. Another local picks up the garda car radio and calls the station: 'Hello, big snack box, over.'

'Who's this?' comes the reply.

The boys are trying to control their laughter: 'Charlie Bird, Charlie Bird.'

A cop emerges from the rumble and chases the lads away. One of them is wearing his garda cap. The squad-car door is open. Someone leans in and lets off the handbrake. The car rolls down the hill and crashes into a World War I monument. No one is hurt, but the boys will pay cash fines on their way to the pub the next day.

Typical Saturday night in a small town in rural Ireland? Well, it was during the boom.

'The Celtic Tiger' is a phrase that was coined in a report for a Morgan Stanley investment bank back in 1994. 'Tiger' was the word often used to describe booming Asian economies. Although lots of things are said to have contributed to the boom (like the rise in house prices, growth in jobs, Ireland opening its doors to workers from new EU member states, and continued foreign direct investment), we reckon it was Jack Charlton. Packie Bonner's save against Romania did more for Ireland than the EU. There was a renewed sense of national pride; the shackles of the church were loosening; the country elected its first female president; U2 were massive; and even Offaly won an All-Ireland. The peak of the boom was 2000 to 2007. Pretty much everyone had a job, disposable income and a loan. See the issue there? We didn't at the time. You can't take someone who's never had money, then give them a load of money and expect them to act responsibly. Apply that to the entire nation of Ireland.

You'd go to the bank and get a mortgage on the back of the value of your own house. Then you'd buy another house for way more than it was worth. Then you'd rent that house out to lads who had loads of money because they were flat-out building houses. We were young at the time and couldn't quite understand how this was supposed to keep going forever. Sure, what did we know?

JS: I used to eat out more than I ate at home. My mother thought nothing of bringing me to The Tower restaurant in Roscrea three times a week to eat minute steak. I was only twelve at the time and I had the body of a beer merchant in his mid-fifties. We'd meet my teachers in there almost every day. They'd have a pint, too, probably spending hundreds of euro a week in there: 'This gravy train isn't going to last forever, but at the moment we're all onboard. Choo-choo!'

You could leave school in fifth year and pull in €1,000 a week on a site. Three years later, you couldn't get a start for love nor money. It was as if someone robbed us; we were all rich, and then we woke up one morning and all our money was gone. The whole country got robbed at the same time.

Skiing holidays were the norm; did ya ever hear the likes of it? My family didn't go skiing, but we did buy a new house. My mam and dad and I went to view this house. We'd seen pictures. It was an average enough house in a nice estate (which is hard to come by in Roscrea). We walked in and it was really warm, with a smell of fresh bread – the whole lot. I thought I was going to walk into the sitting room and find a butler.

In the conservatory there was a bar and a dartboard on the wall. The bar had a sink and two taps, those whiskey dispensers on the back, a nice L-shaped counter, shelves on the wall, photos, Guinness signs, the works. Neither of my parents drink much so I don't know why we were so blown away by it. I reckon the bar added another twenty grand onto the price of the house. I would have preferred a nice heated pool. But there wasn't even a pool in the town. For sixty-five years they were collecting money for a pool in the town and they only got it about four years ago. I don't know if anyone even goes in nowadays. The fun was all in the chase.

Anyway, the bar swung it for us; we had to have this house. The kitchen in our old house was so small that the mother and I couldn't be it in at the same time. You could nearly open the fridge sitting on the couch. So when we saw the bar in the new house, we felt like the Beckhams.

As soon as the ink dried on the contract, the shower started leaking through the sitting-room ceiling. In the first five years we lived there, there was never a pint pulled. My mother ended up putting the bar up for sale on DoneDeal. I think she sold it for €200 quid. We got a pool table instead. There was one corner of the room you couldn't take a shot from, but other than that it was grand.

For some reason I got a bunk bed – actually, for absolutely no reason, I just always wanted a bunk bed. I had no siblings at the time. Maybe it was so my friends could stay over. You wouldn't have got bunk beds before the boom. Older me regretted the decision to get them as I realized it's hard to get a ride in a bunk bed.

During this move, and with the boom in full swing, we got Sky. My dad and I were glued to the soccer. The mother instantly regretted it I'd say.

I had square eyes from the thing. There was a stage when I was able to recite the sports news, I'd have seen it so many times that day. I was watching Conference soccer matches, with the likes of Halifax playing Havant & Waterlooville. Honestly, I would have watched anything. Lads playing kabaddi, did you ever see that? Well, it's basically Indian lads playing tig. And the music channels . . . oh, lad! Thirteen-year-old me staring at Liberty X dancing around in leather. I'll say no more. I got great enjoyment out of telling the lads in school all about my Sky experience, boasting to them about channels like Bravo. At eleven o'clock it turned into some sort of mad European porn station. One minute it was John Fashanu coaching amateur soccer to a bunch of degenerates, the next some German lady was getting drilled. Christ above!

Christmas was unbelievable during the boom. One Christmas I got a pair of football boots worth about €250: Nike Mercurial Vapors, JM9 on the tongue – some nightmare when I was sub at the next game and wearing number 15. The Brazilian striker Ronaldo, or Fat Ronaldo as he became affectionately known, had the same ones. They were bright gold with a black Nike tick. I thought I was the bee's knees. I'd also heard a rumour that they made you run faster, which turned out to be a complete fabrication. I was too fond of eating steak three times a week to move anywhere in a hurry. Money well spent, though. Pure boom.

Another thing going on in our house during the boom was that my mam didn't wash my school shirts. Well, maybe once, depending on how dirty they were. Basically, every week, instead of standing over the sink for hours washing my shirt, she would just buy a new one. It seems a bit excessive now. It wasn't; it was the boom. The guy who worked in our local Shaws must have been delighted when my mother decided this was her approach. I'd say he paid his mortgage out of what the mother was paying out for shirts.

My mam insisted my shirt had to be the whitest in the school. She'd worked in the school shop for a while and had seen the standard of white shirts, or off-white in the case of a lot of students, so she was determined that I be turned out impeccably. She immediately wanted me to stop doing metalwork. I got the cuffs covered in black shite, as she said herself, and it was costing her a fortune in shirts. Also, I was terrible at metalwork. I made a bottle opener once, and she was like, 'What's that?'

I said, 'It's a bottle opener.'

'It doesn't look much like a bottle opener.'

Granted it was shit, but it took me about four days to make. Moral of the story is: metalwork was causing problems for the shirt budget, even in the middle of the boom.

Talking of school, I didn't bring lunch in every day.

Instead, we used to stop in Commerford's shop and get a box of wedges every morning for breakfast and then a salad roll from the deli at lunchtime. We didn't do anything too outrageous during the boom, like buying a villa in Bulgaria like some postmen we heard of. Most of our outlandish behaviour during the Celtic Tiger just came from laziness. No harm done.

JB: *Since Cromwell, the only people who visited Cahir were truckers looking for a steak and a few American tourists. Then around 2002, 500 Polish lads arrived. Our town has a large meat factory, and a lot of my mates' dads worked there, as there was good money to be earned in the boning hall. But when the boom came, they all left the factory overnight and became taxi drivers and contractors.*

The factory was wall-to-wall Eastern Europeans by 2007 and the wages were changed to a flat hourly rate – minimum wage. Our town built a gym and an all-weather pitch. The Polish lads were mad for the gym. Before they came, there was only one man in town who lifted weights, the coalman. He was a beast but couldn't turn his head because his neck was too big. By five o'clock, the new gym would be hopping with lads sporting vests and army haircuts. They'd be shouting at each other and it was all very macho. We heard they all did military service and weren't to be messed with. The only problem was that they dressed like lunatics – white or red tracksuit pants. Sure, how are we not going to poke fun at that? Every Friday and Saturday night outside the nightclub, there'd be war. Lads would come to Mass the next morning with a black eye.

'Who were you fighting?'
'Some Polish lad.'
'Did ya win?'
'Can't remember.'

Get a quick prayer in and a bit of communion and into The Granary Bar to drink fifteen large bottles of cider. Round two next weekend.

The Polish women who arrived a year or two after the lads all seemed very exotic to us. Most of them were fit; they went to the gym as well. This was a completely new concept for Irish women, who perhaps played GAA or went for a walk. I don't think anyone went to the gym before the boom. The Polish women seemed kind of standoffish. They had a look on their face like they were continuously unimpressed with what they saw. To be honest, we weren't very impressive. But lads loved it: 'Look at the big cross head on her. Fair sexy.' Their accents were like something out of a Bond film. When a local man finally started dating a Polish woman, there was some gossip around the town. He came into the pub like he'd just been to the moon. Fellas had a million questions: What was she like here? What did she say there? Do they do it differently in Poland? You'd swear she was from another planet and could breathe underwater or something. After a year or two, no one cared any more. I think they broke up soon after, but he was nearly in the paper as the first man in town to get off with a Polish wan.

JS: When the foreign lads first came to Roscrea, we used to play soccer against them on a Saturday. At first they had hardly a word of English. They'd see us playing soccer in the park and approach saying, 'Soccer . . . Saturday . . . you play?' However many lads we'd gather up, they'd match us and we'd have a game. We were about fifteen and they were in their late twenties, going hell for leather, slide tackles and all, trying to kill us. They'd often be drinking cans. There was one lad, Bondi, and he'd be scuttered, lowering cans of Skol. I don't think his name was actually Bondi, but he kept saying that so that's what we called him. They weren't too bad, but after working ninety-seven hours in the bacon factory that week and downing a slab of cans, they weren't a match for a group of fifteen-year-olds. There was another lad we called Vieri, because he looked exactly like the Italian soccer player Christian Vieri. He didn't play like him, but he taught us how to curse in Polish, which was handy for when I went to work in the factory post-boom.

JB: *At one stage there were over twenty pubs in town. That's about one pub for every hundred people. And they'd be busy all week. It's hard to believe now, but there was live music in a few of the bars, even on Wednesday and Thursday nights. While I was in school, I was able to do a gig and earn €100 a night. I spent it all on CDs. They were about €16 a go. I'd say I put Metallica's kids through college.*

Ireland went up a gear in 1999, when humanity made a breakthrough and started mass production of chicken fillet rolls and breakfast rolls. They had to; we needed the fuel. There were houses being built in the middle of roundabouts. Some were not of the highest standard – flush the toilet and the lights go off. They couldn't build them fast enough. Developers were trying to get in on the act, and if you didn't, you felt like you were missing out. The solution? Throw money at it. Construction wages went up, and if you didn't like your job, you could quit and walk into another one. No wonder we all felt invincible, even if it was completely reckless carry-on.

We talked about the boom on our podcast, and here are a few of our favourite stories listeners sent in:

Back in about 2006 my aunt's husband managed to get his hands on a jet ski from a lad who knew a lad, that kinda job. Anyway, we were from Tullamore and there isn't exactly a whole pile of jet ski lakes around, but it just so happened that it was the time of year that the fields start flooding, so he decided, being the cowboy he was, he'd take it out to the fields where the bypass is, but in those days there was no bypass. Anyway, there were three or four fields connected due to the flooding being so high that he and the lads could speed around. I don't know what people thought when they were driving out the Portlaoise Road though, seeing a few young lads all dressed in the auld construction work gear, no PPE in sight, speeding round a flooded field on a five-grand jet ski. Anyway, as he was speeding round the field, he managed to get the underside of the jet ski stuck on a barbed-wire fence. He went flying off the front at about 60 km/h! The jet ski was done for, and he just got out of the field unscathed, a bit wet, and they all had a laugh. I don't know what happened to the jet ski after. I don't think anyone cared, it being the height of the boom. But it's the most cowboy boom job I've ever heard.

— Ryan

***

I was a private jet and helicopter dealer in those days. I actually sold a private jet to a man in Cashel and two helicopters into Tipperary alone! I have loads of stories relating back to that time. One client's wife insisted her husband buy a helicopter that was €3 million more than the one he was buying, as the electronic step to get into the helicopter was 1.2 inches lower! One chopper was bought using a bank loan for farm machinery.

— Jimmy

***

Lads, in relation to the SSIA and spending. I'm now twenty-five and there's five in my family. When the SSIA came up, my parents thought about spending it or saving it. In the end we spent it. Year one was a seven-day cruise in Alaska, and year two was a ten-day holiday in the States, which included New York, Miami and a five-day Caribbean cruise! God bless Charlie McCreevy. Fast forward two years and we had to get rid of the second car (Fiat Punto) and everything went to shite!

— Jack

***

Well, boys, my aul lad is a bricky and has probably built half of Dublin over the last forty years! I was born in 1990, so I was a teenager for a lot of the Celtic Tiger years. My old man used to have me out working on the building site every summer from the age of fourteen. (The safety inspector was 'told' I was sixteen and had a safe pass . . . wink, wink.) I was getting €350 a week at fourteen for sweeping out houses. I'm barely making that now. It was mad the things that used to go on on those sites! Every labourer, chippy, plumber and apprentice was driving a brand-new Audi! There were more lads hiding than working. Every second house I went to clean would be locked and when you'd peep in the window you'd see lads playing cards. I once even found an electrician asleep in a wardrobe! We were building a huge estate in north Dublin at the time and half the houses were already promised to the workers. Some lads owned two or three houses before they were even built!

I used to go down with my old man every now and then to the bank to get the wages for his gang of lads. The bank manager used to be begging him to take massive loans. It's insane thinking back now. But thankfully the aul lad had a bit of foresight. He grew up on a farm in Monaghan so he lived his life by the principle of 'live within your means'. But nonetheless, there was money being made. The developer, who has been in the news many times since the Tiger, used to land in a massive helicopter every time he'd come to check on the site. They even made a makeshift helipad for him by clearing a pile of clay. Boom times, baby!

— *John*

***

Back in the boom, every time my cousin lost a tooth, the tooth fairy would give him a whopping €50 under his pillow. My cousin was about four or five, so he didn't know what a €50 note was, let alone what to do with it. One time I was having a sleepover at their house and I lost my tooth, so when it came to bedtime I was expecting to be loaded the next morning. That night when the tooth fairy came in, I wasn't fully asleep, so I heard my uncle come in with my aunt. He asked my aunt, 'How much should I give her?' He had a €20 note in his hand and was about to put it under my pillow when my aunt whispered/ shouted, 'No, that's too much.' In my mind I was fuming. Anyway, the next morning I woke up annoyed and excited at the same time. When I looked under my pillow I saw a measly fiver where the €20 should have been. Since then I've never had the opportunity to get another €20, or €50 for that matter, and I didn't think highly of the tooth fairy any more.

— *Éadaoin*

***

So being born in 2000 I don't actually remember much about the boom, but I do remember I was once at my neighbour's Communion, and these neighbours were basically my second family. Anyway, I remember it was nearing the end of the party and I was in the sitting room with my neighbours, when their uncle walked in (mind you, I had never seen or met this man before in my life). This man then started to hand out €50 notes, and in the neighbours' house there were four kids, so straight off the bat he had handed out €200! Then for some reason he handed me one and, sure, I was delighted. Next thing you know one of the neighbours ripped his fifty in half and told his uncle. The uncle said, 'Not to worry,' and threw the fifty in the bin and pulled out a brand-new crisp €50 note. You wouldn't see craic like that today.

— Aoife

***

So, when it comes to the boom, how about three lads sitting at a bar and deciding to go to the Heineken Cup Final? Nothing strange about that, you might say, but hold my beer!

Myself and two other gents decided that we would charter a plane out of Waterford Airport and head to Cardiff for the 2002 final! The plane would take forty-five of us. We contacted the airport and had a meeting with a guy down there and chartered his plane from Waterford to Bristol on the morning of the game. A bus picked us up from Bristol and took us to Cardiff.

It was at this point that my job really kicked in as I had to source the required amount of tickets. Some of the guys that travelled had their own tickets but I got thirty-two of the passengers sorted with tickets from everywhere from schoolboy tickets all the way to corporate BT tickets! The highlight of this was a race against time to the train station in Cardiff and standing in a certain area with a foam thumb over my head to identify myself! Everyone got tickets, and there was even an incident where two fuckers I'd got them for went on and scalped them and went drinking instead!

Munster went and lost the game to Leicester and our flight was the first plane out of Cardiff that evening.

We even had a funny incident with ex-Finance Minister Michael Noonan in the airport where we were offering him a lift home!

We were home and drinking a pint in the Uluru in Waterford watching the highlights of the game at 8 p.m.!

— *Steve K*

***

JS: The roads were the most important thing Ireland gained during the boom. When they were building the motorway from Limerick to Dublin, for the first five years it only went as far as Roscrea. This meant big business for the garage near my house, as it was one of the first ones you'd meet when you got off the motorway.

He must have been cleaning up. It was a tiny shop, and on a Sunday evening you'd be waiting four hours for a pack of chewing gum, the queue would be so long. Like most business owners at the time, he decided he needed a bigger shop, so he moved into a Portakabin while they built it. While they were in the Portakabin, hotdogs were the only food they did. They'd be rotating there on the stand for about fifteen hours. One day I went in to get one, I was only about twelve or thirteen at the time. The owner came into the shop. I'd just seen him outside, putting diesel in a customer's car and changing her oil.

'Can I get a hotdog?' I asked.

He replied, 'Is it straight for the chop?'

'Well, I'm going to eat it, yeah.'

He picked up the bun and sausage with his bare hands, no tin foil, no tissues, straight out to me. There was oil on the sausage. I was nearly high off the fumes. But I ate it. I'd no choice. Food safety wasn't an issue; it was the boom. Thank God he hired proper staff for the new shop. Soon after the grand opening of the new shop, the motorway reached Limerick. Hotdog sales collapsed and there are no major queues in the massive store now.

JB: *Dublin got the Spire on O'Connell Street, Wexford got the National Opera House, our town got an industrial estate and a massive housing estate that I'd still get lost in if I went up there now.*

The auld summer fair that was usually a trad session and a donkey derby turned into a rock concert and also featured a fireworks display that cost five grand to put on. We heard of people getting 150 per cent mortgages, shopping trips to New York, buying property abroad, and some fella in Dublin apparently hired Girls Aloud to play at his daughter's twenty-first. Property prices peaked around 2007. By 2010 there were reportedly 300,000 vacant homes in Ireland and 600 ghost estates. In 2012 almost 50,000 young Irish people emigrated. At one stage in my early twenties, I was the only player from our county-minor-winning side still living in town. Cahir even appeared in an RTÉ TV documentary about emigration called Departure Day. *The programme featured young Irish people who were being forced to emigrate and followed them in the week leading up to the big departure. Two lads I went to school with appeared in the documentary. It wasn't Cahir's finest hour. The opening scene was the two lads drinking cans down the local graveyard, saying that they were going to Australia because there was no work locally. Everyone said the town came across as grim. The surviving publicans wrote a furious letter to someone about it.*

Nowadays in Cahir the nightclub is closed up, although we still hold out hope that someday it will reopen and the town will be hopping again. One thing that will be missing from the club will be that drum kit signed by U2. I later found out that a local lad had taken the signed skins and replaced them with his own old ones, and he even wrote a few squiggles for authenticity. I mean, would you recognize Bono's signature?

JS: During the boom years Roscrea wasn't exactly transformed into the Las Vegas of Munster. It wasn't drowning in state-of-the-art facilities; our local soccer club didn't even have a dressing room. We togged out behind an oak tree. The most exciting thing I remember from back then was that one time a man barricaded himself into his house with a load of gas cylinders and said he was going to blow them up. RTÉ News came down. They had the whole street cordoned off for about two days. Every camera in Ireland must have been there. Live bulletins from Roscrea – we couldn't believe it. They had to evacuate the whole street. In the end he handed himself in. Turns out the bomb he built was 'elaborate but incapable of actually being detonated', according to the guards. That's about as exciting as our town got in the boom.

What did Roscrea get out of the boom? I'm fairly sure at one stage the two main streets were entirely made up of pubs and bookies. That's about all we got, not that the people who were flying high during that period would see it that way. The boom was like a big night out – it seemed like great craic at the time but the comedown and hangover were brutal. Hopefully we'll have learned our lessons by the time the next boom comes around.

ACKNOWLEDGEMENTS

Thanks for reading the book, hi. Hopefully we can buy a hot tub off the back of it. We hope ye enjoyed it and if you think that a particular story was about you, then you're wrong. We promise.

JS: To my fiancée, Annie, my mother, Trish, dad, David and sister, Abi, thanks for putting up with me. I hope ye don't mind all the stories I've told about ye in this book, although it's probably too late if you're reading this.

JB: I think my family want to remain anonymous, but they're sound out anyway.

Thanks a million to:

Our management, Joe and Paul, and the team at CWB.

Big James Hayes (AKA Moto Moto) for keeping us alive and safe while we're on the road.

Our podcast producer and one of our best friends, Maura. Thanks for being a legend and keeping us on the straight and narrow, off and on air.

Eoin Ennis, for all your hard work in making us look and sound good. Not an easy job, to say the least.

Neil the intern, we bet you wish you'd done your internship in some posh Dublin office.

Cecil and Jack Carter, for their anecdotes and skills at our live productions.

Brendan 'The King' Fitzpatrick, for driving us around and eating scones.

Our friends, for jumping in on sketches and being sound. Ye give us so many laughs. We don't get to see ye as much as we'd like.

Cahir GAA, for all yer support. Never stop being mental, ye legends.

All the girls in the office: Tina, Susan, Fabritiza, Janine, Moesha, Sabrina the Teenage Witch, April O'Neil, Dirty Mike and the boys, Buffy, Monica, Angela, Pamela, Sandra and Rita, and as we continue, you know they getting sweeter.

To all the guys at Big Mo's Tavern Studio and John Kendrick Records, your guidance and patience has been unbelievable.

Also thanks a million to everyone who is part of the extended 2 Johnnies team:

A&R man – Ger Hally

Front of house – Niall Halley

Special effects – Jerry Tarrent

Head of casting – Dan Costigan

Scripting – Brian Dolan

Head of Jaimeens – Denis

Transport – Ryan Murphy

Modelling and image consultant – The Choc Ice

Head of sucklers – Sean O'Connor

Financial controller – Jamsey Walsh

Security – Aidan Casey

Head of keys – Larry Q

Skinny Tracksuits sponsored by Jim Deluxe.

To the staff of Quinn's Killenaule, thanks for the pound of corned beef, we owe you €2.70.

Thanks to 'The Chicken' for a great day of stories. None of them could be published. We'll be back.

But most importantly, thank you to everyone who has bought this book, come to our shows, listened to our podcasts, bought our music and watched our sketches. Ye are the reason we get to do what we love. We owe ye all big time. The pints are on us.

Lastly, we hope ye had a laugh reading this, life is too short. Our aim, as always, is to cheer people up and get a conversation going. All we ask is that you don't take yourself too seriously and that you're sound to everyone.

Big love,
The 2 Johnnies.

P.S. Keep chicken rolls at €4.

QUIZ ANSWERS

1. Gaelic Athletic Association.

2. Martin Storey.

3. County Clare.

4. A cow milked.

5. Mícheál Ó Muircheartaigh.

6. The Croke Park Hotel.

7. Johnny Pilkington.

8. Larry O'Gorman.

9. Babs Keating.

10. Hayes Hotel.

11. It's debatable.

12. Terence.

13. Cork's Teddy McCarthy won the hurling and football for Cork in 1990.

14. Tipp's John Leahy was so impressive in the 1994 league campaign that he won an All Star despite being injured for the entire championship.

15. Local barber and Roscommon football fanatic Paddy Joe Burke climbed the stadium wall while his wife held the ladder. At 12.01 a.m. on New Year's Day 2000, he ran onto the pitch and blasted a ball into the back of an open goal.